DATE DUE

GAYLORD		PRINTED IN U.S.A.

SCIENCE AND CULTURE TEXTS
JOSEPH HUSSLEIN, S.J., Ph.D., GENERAL EDITOR

RELIGION AND LEADERSHIP

Religion and
Leadership

By DANIEL A. LORD, S.J.

National Organizer of the Sodality of Our Lady
for the United States • Director of the Students'
Spiritual Leadership Movement

THE BRUCE PUBLISHING COMPANY
CHICAGO · MILWAUKEE · NEW YORK

Imprimi potest
S. H. HORINE, S.J.
Praepositus Provincialis Provinciae Missourianae

Nihil obstat
H. B. RIES
Censor librorum

Imprimatur
✠ SAMUEL A. STRITCH
Archiepiscopus Milwaukiensis
July 19, 1933

Affectionately and Gratefully Dedicated
to my Mother
To Whom, Under God,
I Owe My Precious Faith

PREFACE BY THE GENERAL EDITOR

RELIGION AND LEADERSHIP is the first of a series of religion texts that have arisen out of the very heart of our modern college life. They embody the desires, aspirations, and ideals of representative groups of teachers of religion from various parts of the United States, on whose initiative these books have been written.

Choice of subjects, determination of the general plan, and selection of authors rested with the experienced men and women teachers constituting these discussion groups, but the distinctive development of the separate works has necessarily been the contribution of the writers themselves. Strict uniformity of method was rather avoided than sought. This lends to each volume a freshness and attractiveness of its own, and prevents the monotony which else must result for the student in passing from one course to another. Each book will prove for him a new discovery, filled with its own stimulating interest and adventure.

It is well that the very first of these volumes should deal with the subject of Catholic leadership. Mankind, it has been observed, accomplishes nothing save through the initiative of its leaders. The masses imitate and follow. The quality of the guides to whom they give allegiance in any epoch determines the civilization of the times. The world today is filled with what our Lord so strikingly called, blind leaders of the blind.

The responsibility of preparing for true leadership descends as a solemn obligation upon the Catholic college men and women the moment they enter the sacred precincts of the Catholic school, where there is one Head Master, Christ. Their battles of the future will be won under His direction in the classrooms of today. Their contributions to the welfare of a society that so greatly needs their aid, and to the increase of the Kingdom of God on earth, will depend on the studies they here pursue and the spirit that prompts their labors now.

But the present book is more than merely a splendid inspiration to Catholic leadership. It is a complete orientation course in religion. It is a survey of Catholic doctrine and practice which other groups may find equally useful to answer their own special needs.

Two things are imperative for the Catholic leader: a perfect knowledge of the Faith, and a thorough training in its application under present-day conditions. To make this possible is the purpose of this entire series of religion texts. That they imply work is true, but that

ix

is their virtue. No ill-prepared, haphazard, careless methods will suffice. More is called for here than the mere distillation of knowledge, however pure it may come from the teacher's alembic, into the passive brain of the student.

The focal point of all Christian teaching, the scintillating core of the whole system of Catholic education, is the religion class. With it no other course in the curriculum can compare in importance — except insofar as it also ministers to the same end. It is the opportunity of opportunities for teacher and pupil.

In the early Church long and conscientious preparation was called for before the neophyte was admitted through the door of baptism into the fold of the Church. Only then "the Mystery of Faith," the Holy Eucharist, was revealed to him. He was entering into the possession of something that he well knew was beyond all price. He was freely embracing what might mean to him the sacrifice of everything else he held dear upon earth, and what, with no remote possibility, might bring him in the end rack, burning, and the grinding to death by the teeth of wild beasts in the Roman amphitheater. But through all these things he trusted to pass, by the grace of God, to the eternal union with Him. It was worth the price.

Religion then had a sublime significance for him. It was in truth and in reality a matter of life and death. The learning of it was his most serious occupation. It should be no less for us. It is worth a hundredfold the efforts it may cost. Especially must this hold true of the orientation course that is to give the keynote to the student's life.

For many years the author of this book has been widely known in collegiate circles as one of the most inspiring and energizing forces that have entered into the Catholic student's life. The skill and method of his work, the contagion and enthusiasm of his zeal, are wrought into this important volume. It has the distinction of being issued as the first of the Science and Culture Texts, intimately related to the Science and Culture Series, and is to be followed at once by its companion volumes, *The Catholic Church and the Modern Mind* and *Christian Life and Worship*.

JOSEPH HUSSLEIN, S.J., PH.D.
General Editor, Science and Culture Texts

Feast of Our Lady of Mount Carmel, 1933.
St. Louis University,
St. Louis, Missouri.

AUTHOR'S PREFACE

In the very happy years of my connection with the Students' Spiritual Leadership Movement under the direction of The Sodality of Our Lady, religious education has been a consuming interest. This is due to the fact that every time a group of college (or high-school, for that matter) teachers met, or a group of students gathered in national or local conventions, the subject of the religion class and textbooks was sure to raise its head.

The interest of the students in religion was undoubted. The desire of the faculty to improve that subject which is the very reason for the existence of our Catholic schools, was also obvious.

In many a faculty meeting in every part of the country we thrashed out the subject as well as we could. We encouraged the students in the presence of their instructors to tell us what they wanted in their religion course and what they thought a religion course should give them.

As these sometimes warm and always most interesting discussions proceeded, it seemed to me that one thing was obvious. No place in the whole course of their studies did the students get a comprehensive idea of the purpose of Catholic education nor any unified presentation of that most beautifully articulated system of thought and belief and devotion and philosophy and practice that we know as the Catholic Church.

In addition, there seemed to be, among both students and faculty, a conviction that between religion classes in high school and those in college there was not nearly enough difference in content or approach.

So for two summers in succession, we gathered groups of these interested teachers of religion to talk about just what could be done to give the student early in his college days this sweeping view of religion. And we discussed in detail by what ways religion in college could be made distinctly collegiate in character and totally different in approach from religion as taught in the high schools. The ideas and suggestions these groups gave were most valuable.

Then through long and delightful winter evenings, Father Robert Bakewell Morrison and Father William J. McGucken and members of the staff of the Sodality Central Office and myself gathered and planned for a series of college religion texts which would, we hope embody the things both teachers and students seemed to want.

An outline for three texts was drawn up. This was submitted to groups of teachers and students for their approval or criticism and suggestion.

The results of all this are to be found in the three texts now appearing, with this volume as the first. Father Morrison has written the second; Father Gerald Ellard, the third.

Whether the books will meet with the response we hope for is decidedly a question. Whether they will do for the teaching of religion what we pray they will do, is just another question. We can only assure the teachers and the students both that into the books we have put our best thought and planning. We have tried to face the problems of the religion classroom and the difficulties in the mind of the modern student and solve them.

We can only say that we offer these books with a deep appreciation of the splendid interest in their most essential subject that has been displayed by the religion professors and instructors in our Catholic colleges. And we can add that we offer the books to the students out of a deep affection for them and a real desire to see them finish their Catholic colleges, intellectually sure of their faith, convinced that it has the answer to the world's needs, and already intensely engrossed in the cause of Catholic action.

Most of all, we hope and pray that the religion classes will convince the student that religion is the most inspiring subject in the world, and that true religion is not a series of burdensome "don'ts" and "mustn'ts," but the enthusiastic following of the world's Supreme Leader, Jesus Christ, under the protecting smile of the world's loveliest woman, Mary.

The Catholic college student of the present is, we hope and pray, the sure and trustworthy and inspiring leader in the cause of Catholic Action tomorrow.

My thanks for invaluable help in the production of this text goes to the students of the Summer Schools of Catholic Action, to the members of the Staff of the Sodality Central Office, notably Father J. Roger Lyons, Father George McDonald, and Miss Dorothy J. Willmann, and to Sister Marie Clyde of Webster College.

DANIEL A. LORD, S.J

Passion Sunday, 1933.

AUTHOR'S FOREWORD

This text is primarily offered to college students in Catholic colleges. Study groups, however, may find it of value in directing the course of study discussions outside of classrooms or schools.

If used in freshman college year, it is to be considered an orientation course in religion and is to be given to all students attending the Catholic college, whether Catholic or non-Catholic.

The early chapters are designed on the basis of an hour's lecture, followed by an hour of quiz, of problems, and of discussion of the reading assignments. Later chapters will require more time. At least two hours' study will be needed for every hour of class.

The book is intended to be used almost as a workbook or classroom guide. It is the basis around which the instructor builds his lecture. It must be supplemented by the research, thought, discussion, and reading of the student.

This research, thought, discussion, and reading on the part of the student is fundamental in importance. The more the classes resemble effective and active seminars or study clubs, the better the book is being used and the better the results which the instructor may expect from his class.

Notes will be carefully taken from the instructor's lecture and from the answers to the problems and discussions brought out in class.

The problems and discussions follow logically from the matter suggested in the text. They are not, however, directly answered in the text. They cannot be answered without thought and sometimes research on the part of the student. For this reason they are an essential part of the class technique.

These problems and discussions may be assigned one to each member of the class, or where classes are large, one to a group of members. In some cases where the questions are rather simple, two or more questions may be assigned to an individual or a group. Written answers to these questions may be required from the class.

Written assignments based on the suggested discussions are advised.

Readings should be assigned to accompany every lesson of the text. In addition, quarterly book reports are expected of all students.

Most of the subjects are not exhausted in the text. The course is to be regarded as a survey course and not a comprehensive course. It outlines for the student, viewpoints, standards, bases, fundamentals which will be much more fully developed as the college courses in religion, philosophy, history, science, and literature proceed. This text sketches the purposes and objectives of the college course, and the high points of dogmatic, moral, and devotional religion and philosophy.

For this reason, the class should be warned against protracted discussions of minor questions that impede the general sweep of the course. Broad outlines are given which can be filled out only with comprehensive and intensive study.

D. A. L., S.J.

CONTENTS

     Enrollment in a Catholic College. Distinctive Fea-
     tures. Erection at a Tremendous Sacrifice. Cath-
     olic College Created for Love of Principles. God
     Recognized in Education. Divine Teaching Com-
     mission of Catholic Church. Present Need for a
     Catholic College. Problems and Discussions. Sug-
     gested Readings.

     1. FAITH. Two Sources of Human Knowledge. Ex-
     perience Deepened and Broadened Through Col-
     lege. Faith from Authority. Faith, the Divine Vir-
     tue. Gift of Faith Leads to Salvation. Revelation
     Must be Studied. Unique Position Regarding Faith
     Held by Catholic Students. Two Possibilities for
     Catholic College Student. Problems and Discus-
     sions. Suggested Readings.

     2. A SHINING EXAMPLE. Tribute of Christ to His
     Followers. What Christ Expects of Catholics. A
     Tribute, a Prophecy, and a Warning by Christ and
     St. Paul. Catholic College Student More Than One
     of Followers of Christ. Exemplary Conduct De-
     manded from Catholic Student. Shining Example
     of Catholic Student. Problems and Discussions.
     Suggested Readings.

     3. USE OF OPPORTUNITIES. Purposes of College
     Educations. Two Types of Students. Learning De-
     finite Facts. Education Most Valuable for Oneself.
     How to Learn More Later During Life. Important
     Considerations in Learning to Work. Work and So-
     cial Life. Supernaturalizing Work. Problems and
     Discussions. Suggested Readings.

Chapter I

WHY A CATHOLIC COLLEGE?

I. The basic fact to be accepted by the class is: *You are enrolled in a* **Catholic College.** Why?
 A. Perhaps through the *choice of parents* or guardians.
 B. Perhaps because of its *proximity* and accessibility.
 C. Perhaps for some *personal reason,* such as advice of friends, sports, social life, prestige.
 D. Perhaps because it *is Catholic.*

II. Whatever the reason, the newcomer recognizes that this **Catholic College** has **distinctive features:**
 A. *A cross* is over the main building, the standard of a crucified God.
 B. *A chapel,* open all day, is the center of the college life; with the Blessed Sacrament reserved all day; regular opportunity for Mass; services for the students; confessionals, etc.
 C. *Priestly and religious teachers* compose the large part of the faculty; the college itself is controlled by a religious community or by the diocese.
 D. *Some religion courses* are required and additional courses are offered.
 E. *Scholastic philosophy* (a distinct and different way of looking at life and regarding its meaning, conduct, objective) is taught.
 F. *Catholic thought and viewpoint* permeate the courses.
 G. *The student body* is predominantly Catholic.
 H. *Religious societies and organizations* are stressed in addition to the usual student organizations.
 I. *A yearly retreat* is given.
 J. *The success of the Alumni (Alumnæ)* is measured less in terms of visible success than by Christ's standard: "What does it profit a man to gain the whole world and suffer the loss of his own soul?"
 K. *The teachings of Christ* and the guidance of the Catholic Church are freely accepted.

1

III. This College has been erected at **tremendous sacrifice:**
   A. While state colleges offer (in most cases) to their students free tuition, the students and parents pay from *$100,000* to *$1,000,000 or more a year* to make this college possible.

Note: They do this in addition to paying the taxes that make possible the free tuition in state schools.

   B. The faculty (religious, priests) give their *free services* and "the endowment in man power."

Note: Standardizing agencies and groups accept this free service as real endowment. If paid, each faculty member would receive from $1,200 to $5,000 a year. From this fact their donation to the college can be judged.

   C. *The buildings and equipment* were not provided by state taxes (paid by Catholics as well as non-Catholics) nor by large endowments (which are rare in Catholic colleges) but had their origin:
      1. In the *labor* and *devoted planning* of religious community or diocese;
      2. In an *actual financial investment* by them with heavy burdens of debt and worry.

IV. All this implies that the Catholic college must be created for **love of principles:**
   A. **Educated Catholics** who want to be **leaders** must, beyond their training of mind and body (brain and brawn):
      1. Be *trustworthy:* Untrustworthy leaders are dangerous leaders, selfish, ignorant, "misleading."
         a) *Intellectually sure* of what they believe, know, and attempt to do;
         b) *Morally sound* in every phase of conduct.
      2. *Know themselves thoroughly:*
         a) In their relationship with *themselves;* as private individuals.
         b) In their relationship *with others;* in business, marriage, man-to-man, man-to-woman aspects.
         c) In their relationship *with the State;* as citizens.
         d) In their relationship *with God.*
      3. Be impressed with **the importance of:**
         a) *All truth,* natural and supernatural, realizing that

cleverness is not wisdom, smartness is not knowledge, quickness and glibness are not depth.

b) *Human souls.* If bodies die, while souls are immortal; if beyond this world there is another; if men are to be judged eternally on the basis of their conduct; then souls are tremendously important.

Note: These "ifs" cease to be mere "ifs" when treated fully in philosophy and religion courses.

c) *God in the human life,* as Creator, Father, Coöperator, Savior, Sanctifier, Benefactor, Judge, Rewarder, and Punisher.

Note: To ignore these questions, vitally important and of deep concern to all men, is to set a man adrift in life, not sure of his ultimate destination, purpose, or controlling forces. And education which leaves a man ignorant of these questions and their answers, misses the main points.

4. Be students, and *followers of really great leaders:*
   a) *Christ,* the perfect model of manhood.
   b) *The saints,* not as pious visionaries, but as heroes, pioneers, thinkers, artists, organizers, heroines; e.g., Paul, Patrick, Boniface, Augustine, Stephen and Sebastian; Cyril, Aquinas, Bonaventure; Francis, Dominic, Bernard, Ignatius; Agnes, Catherine, Joan of Arc, Theresa.
   c) *Great servants of humanity,* Charlemagne, A'Becket, Michelangelo, Beethoven, Louis IX, Pasteur.

V. **God has a right to a place** in educational institutions.
   A. If God created the world . . . If men are His children . . . If He is the one who directs our destinies and is to be our eternal reward . . . then education that eliminates Him is education that omits man's most important relationship and elements.

VI. **The Catholic Church** received from Christ a divine teaching commission: "Go ye therefore . . . and teach all nations."
   A. Hence the Catholic Church has the *obligation* of teaching and the consequent right to build the colleges in which this teaching can be carried on in accord with the needs of the times.

VII. Today especially the **Catholic college** is needed because:
  A. The world is *filled with leaders,* educated, but:
    1. *Mentally vague* and indecisive and uncertain.
    2. *Morally unsound* and uncertain and positively evil.
    3. Leading the *world terribly astray.*
  B. *The chief attacks* upon religion and morality are being made by intellectually educated men who must be met by intellectually educated men.
  C. In a world torn by *warring opinions,* the Catholic Church presents a *system* of thought and life *logical, sane, livable, beautiful.* Its followers must not only live that life but know what it means and why it is true and beautiful.
    Difficulty: I have a parochial-school training, a Catholic high-school training, and come from a Catholic home. Hence, I do not need Catholic college training.
    Response: 1. The attack on faith and morals today is literary, philosophical, scientific. The answers to these attacks can hardly be learned except at college.
    2. The world is vastly ignorant of Catholic truth. It ignores it. Its atmosphere is one of chill neglect. Hence, men and women are needed who can present the Catholic position to the world.
    Difficulty: Success in life depends upon my training in science, literature, practical subjects. The Catholic college stresses religion and philosophy, not connected with success.
    Response: 1. Ultimate success is not measured merely in fortune and fame, but in a fully developed life, correct in all its relationships, chief among which is my relationship to God, to my soul, to moral law, to eternity.
    2. The Catholic college gives all that other colleges give of science, literature, etc., plus the otherwise omitted elements of religion and correct philosophy. It neglects nothing essential for life and adds what is essential for eternal life.

Problems and Discussions

1. "Man is a creature composed of body and soul." If this statement is true, why does the Catholic college give the only correct type of college education?
2. How many Catholic colleges are there in the United States today? What is their enrollment? What financial investment does this represent? If their teachers were actually paid by the state taxes, what would this cost the state?
3. What has a student the right to expect from a Catholic college education?

4. Discuss the symbolism of the Cross over the college buildings; of the crucifix in the college classrooms? Do they seem to you out of place in educational institutions?
5. Discuss what is meant by a trustworthy leader. Can you give instances of such leaders and of their contrary?
6. What importance has a correct attitude toward life in a leader?
7. What particular intellectual qualities make an untrained or badly trained Catholic leader a peril to those he leads?
8. What answer could be given to a high-school graduate who says, "I'm going to a non-Catholic college; it can't hurt my faith"?
9. Discuss what you consider to be essential elements in a well-rounded education.
10. Debate: The non-Catholic world is ignorant of the Church rather than opposed to it.
11. What elements of sacrifice have gone into the building of your College?
12. Discuss the Catholic who selects his college only, or chiefly because of its social prestige.
13. What effect upon future life can we expect if a college has deprived a Catholic of his faith? If it graduates him educated in all except his faith?
14. Explain to a non-Catholic why the educated Catholic firmly believes in necessity of Catholic education.

Suggested Readings

PAMPHLETS

The Queen's Work Press:
Murder in the Classroom, Lord, S.J.

MAGAZINE REFERENCES

America:
"The Catholic College Student," Vol. 25, p. 222.
"A War for Catholic Education," Vol. 16, p. 431.
"Religion in the School," Vol. 22, p. 351.
"Fruits of a Non-Catholic College," Vol. 34, p. 241.
"Death in the Non-Catholic College," Vol. 26, p. 93.
"The Catholic Boy and His College," Vol. 23, p. 523.
Commonweal:
"What is a Catholic Education," Vol. 23, p. 70.
"Catholic Colleges as Civic Assets," Vol. 7, p. 1142.
"Religion and Education," Vol. 2. Oct. 14.

BOOKS

Coler, *Two and Two Make Four* (Beattys).
Sheehy, *Christ and the Catholic College* (Wagner).

Chapter II

QUALITIES EXPECTED OF A CATHOLIC COLLEGE STUDENT OR ANY CATHOLIC LEADER

1. Faith

I. There are **two great sources of all human knowledge**: **Experience** and **Authority**.

II. **Experience:** Through college this is to be deepened and broadened:

    A. *Scientific data,* tested, investigated, experimented with, studied, personally proved, increase one's factual knowledge.

    B. *Historical data,* when they bring students in contact with first-hand documents, and proved facts.

    C. *The senses are quickened,* the mind made more alert, the appreciation developed through contact with literature and the arts.

    D. *The critical faculties* are developed to distinguish true from false, and to make accurate appraisals of correct and incorrect, through experience with philosophy, literary appreciation, contact with masters in science, thought, creative art.

Note: The world is full of false intellectual and artistic and scientific values; hence, the importance of learning to appreciate and know correctly true and false. The ability to evaluate facts is more important from our experience than a mere knowledge of facts.

Hence: Study at college is:

    1. Not merely the acquirement of facts.

    2. But also the development through experience of the ability to judge, appraise, evaluate facts throughout life.

        a) All this is carefully cared for by the college course.

        b) What is actually gained from the course depends upon the student.

III. From **Authority,** i.e., the word of another, comes forth **Faith** — the acceptance of knowledge on the word of another.

    A. **Natural Faith** is one of the commonest means of obtaining knowledge. It may be based, for instance, on:

1. *Personal facts,* concerning parentage, birthplace, early history before consciousness, told by others.
2. Facts gained through *newspapers,* foreign and home news that are taken on the word of reporters, correspondents.
3. *Historical and biographical facts,* such as are usually taken from historians or biographers whose sources are not investigated by the ordinary reader.
4. *Geography,* concerned with places unvisited by individual who accepts the account of the geographer.
5. *Ordinary facts,* passed from friend to friend and never checked up.
6. *Most scientific data.*
   a) The ordinary reader accepts the facts of science on the word of a scientist.
   b) The specialist checks up and investigates only his particular field. He accepts the data of other fields on the word of others.
7. Hence, we live surrounded by natural faith, the acceptance of facts on the word of someone else.

B. **Divine Faith** is the transference of this natural human acceptance of truth on the word of a fellow man to:
1. *The word of God.*
2. *The word of Christ,* His divine Son.
3. *The word of the Church,* His divinely appointed teacher and representative. (This last is technically "ecclesiastical" faith.)

Note: All intelligent men should recognize that there are some things beyond the range of human exploration that either simply cannot be known or else in the present condition of mankind are not going to be known by everyone with facility, with firm assurance, and with no admixture of error without the help of divine revelation. Catholics recognize among these things facts which are:

1. *Knowable both from experience and reasoning and also knowable from faith,* through the acceptance of revelation, e.g., the existence of God, of souls, of immortality.
2. *Known entirely owing to revelation* and by means of faith, e.g., the Trinity, grace, the Incarnation.

Note: This would be a poor and limited world if men could explore and

know it all. No man has ever done this for even the earth. The world beyond this one would be equally poor if much of it were not beyond the
range of experience and reasoning.

IV. **Faith,** i.e., the divine virtue, by whose acts we accept things as
true through the word of God (because He has revealed them
who can neither be deceived nor will deceive us, *is a gift of God*).
It puts us in possession of knowledge to which we have no natural
claim, whether it be that our natural powers would fail in attain-
ing to the fact or merely would not reach the fact in the same
sure and advantageous way. This virtue is a free gift of God. It is
a virtue required for our salvation.

　　A. But all the facts which we come to know through the exer-
　　cise of this divine, infused virtue of Faith:

　　　　1. *Accord adequately with our reason.* They may be beyond
　　　　our experience and reason; they never contradict or oppose
　　　　our reason, e.g., faith in the existence of God (God's revela-
　　　　tion of His own existence) is in accord with our scientific
　　　　and philosophical proofs that God exists.

　　　　2. *Fit in with our desires and inclinations and nature.* Hence,
　　　　the facts of faith are beautiful and befitting ("becoming"),
　　　　e.g., from faith we know of grace and the supernatural life.
　　　　From reason and experience we know we are not merely
　　　　animals; we are unwilling to be merely animals. Faith teach-
　　　　es us that grace gives us a supernatural life like that of God
　　　　and His angels.

　　　　3. *Are either proved by reason or, at least, reason can find
　　　　nothing contradictory in them.* Through faith we are taught
　　　　of immortality; but immortality is also proved by reason,
　　　　as, for example, by argument based on the fact that human
　　　　nature craves perfect happiness, i.e., happiness that never
　　　　will end.

V. **The Gift of Faith,** i.e., the divine virtue by means of which we
hold fast to things beyond experience and reason, and other things,
too, all vouched for by God is normally given the Catholic, in such
a manner as leads to salvation:

　　A. *At Baptism:* undeserved, unmerited, yet necessary for reach-
　　ing heaven (a man cannot go to heaven if he does not in some
　　way believe); faith is given when the Catholic becomes a child
　　of God.

B. *Early home training and Catholic education* develop faith.

C. *Prayer,* the reception of the sacraments, correct reading, all increase faith.

VI. To be properly appreciated and developed, **revelation must be studied,** intellectually assimilated, practiced, and firmly held by an act of one's will. *Faith is:*

    A. *"The Faith,"* i.e., a beautiful and elaborate structure requiring thought and study.

    B. *The preambles of Faith, i.e., a chain of facts* proved reasonably and persuasively.

    C. *The infused theological virtue, i.e., a gift* that is *preserved* and developed:

        1. *By practice.* (More important than the theory of football, piano, airplaning, is practice. This holds in measure for faith.) Acts of faith, actions inspired by faith are essential.

        2. *By study.* The act of faith is not an emotional experience but an intellectual grasp on difficult facts.

        3. *By correct reading.* A vast library has been developed explaining and defending the facts revealed by faith.

Note: Most of the violent attacks against the Faith are based on moral and emotional grounds. Men dislike something revealed by God, e.g., God's attitude toward marriage, the fact of sin and man's responsibility for sin, and they argue against it. They object to the Ten Commandments, so they say there is no God to give them. They want freedom, so they question the right of Christ to curtail this.

VII. Catholic students hold a **unique position** regarding faith:

    A. *Doubt,* uncertainty, partial knowledge, disbelief grows more characteristic of the world of *non-Catholic students.*

    B. Because of a Catholic education, the *Catholic students are expected* by their associates, Catholic and non-Catholic:

        1. *To know their faith.*

        2. *To be able to explain* and defend their faith.

        3. *To live their faith.*

    C. *They received freely* and without effort what converts gained often with immense difficulty and sacrifice and struggle.

    D. They belong to *races that became martyrs* and died rather than give up that faith:

        1. Not merely the *early Christian* martyrs.

        2. But the *Irish* of Cromwell's and Penal days.

3. *English* Catholics of the reign of the late Tudors and Stuarts.

4. *German Catholics* during the Kulturkampf, and *French* during the Revolution and the laws against religion.

5. *Mexico* and *Spain* and *Russia* today.

VIII. A Catholic college student has either of **two possibilities:**

A. *To live with a faith that is misunderstood* or half understood, timidly held, hesitant, because it has never been mastered, grasped, and proved to his satisfaction.

B. *Or to live with a proved,* understood, intelligent faith, sure of his position and meeting attacks confidently because of complete and satisfactory knowledge.

The college course in religion and philosophy prepares the student for the second condition and possibility.

The student must decide whether to *use* the course or not.

Problems and Discussions

1. Give instances of natural faith taken from the daily papers, from some popular scientific book, from history, from geography, from some recent conversation in which you have taken part.

2. Answer a man who says: "I only accept what I have experienced and proved."

3. Would you agree with the statement that all loss of faith starts with loss of morals? Give instances from your reading or experience of history (names, unless publicly known, omitted) to demonstrate your answer.

4. If the following statements were not facts revealed through the faith, would they still be beautiful, reasonable, dignified, suited to man's desires and nature? Give reason for your answer.

   a) By baptism we become the sons and daughters of a Heavenly Father.

   b) My soul will never die.

   c) Heaven and purgatory and earth are bound together in a great empire called the Communion of Saints.

   d) By prayer man can affect the affairs and destiny of the world.

   e) God so loved the world that He stays with it in the tabernacle.

   f) God gave groping man an infallible helper and teacher called the Church.

   g) My body is the temple of the Holy Spirit.

   h) God made marriage a sacred and holy thing and gives special graces and helps to young married couples.

   i) My will is free.

5. Do you, on the other hand, find anything beautiful and dignified or in accord with man's true nature and desires in the following dogmas of unbelief:
   a) Men are merely improved animals.
   b) When the ones I love die, I shall never see them again.
   c) Fate, in the form of natural law, rules the world and prayer cannot change it.
   d) Men have no free will; they cannot influence their destiny.
   e) There is no infallible teacher to help men in their struggle for truth.
   f) Marriage is like the mating of the beasts.
6. Why did St. James speak violently against men whose faith failed to show itself in their conduct?
7. Debate: Converts more deeply appreciate the faith than born Catholics.
8. Discuss this statement: In times of persecution, men cling passionately to their faith; in times of prosperity, they give it up for things their martyred ancestors would have despised.
9. Why is faith listed as the first quality expected of a Catholic college student?
10. Discuss the statement: The attacks upon faith common today necessitate a deeper study and clearer knowledge of the proofs and beauty and reasonableness of faith.

Suggested Readings

PAMPHLETS

The Queen's Work Press:
* *My Faith and I*, Lord, S.J.
  The Best Best Seller, Lord, S.J.
The Paulist Press:
  Agnosticism, Gerard.
  Belief in God and in Religion, O'Brien.
  Reason and Religion, Lummer, C.P.
  I Wish I Could Believe, Baldwin.
The Catholic Truth Society:
  From Synagogue to Church, Ratisbonne.
  How I Became a Catholic, Bull.
  Why Must I Have Any Religion At All, Bevan.
  Faith and Reason, Vaughan, S. J.

BOOKS

Knox, *Broadcast Minds* (Sheed & Ward).
Chesterton, *The Superstitions of the Skeptic* (Herder).
Claudel, *Letters to a Doubter* (Boni).

Chapter III

QUALITIES EXPECTED OF A CATHOLIC COLLEGE STUDENT OR ANY CATHOLIC LEADER

2. A Shining Example

I. **Christ pays tribute** to His followers, and adds a prophecy and warning in His famous phrases:

"You are a city seated upon a mountain."

"So let your light shine before men that they may see your good works and glorify your Father who is in heaven."

"You are the salt of the earth."

II. **Catholics** in general are expected by Christ to be:

A. *Conspicuous as a city* lifted above the plain and placed upon the top of a mountain.

B. *A light,* for all to see; a guide to lead them safely; a beacon to travelers.

C. *Salt* of the earth, the preservative, the seasoner.

St. Paul adds another idea to this general idea:

Spectaculum facti sumus angelis et hominibus, "We have become a spectacle for angels and men" (I Cor. iv. 9).

A spectacle: Something for the crowds to look at, admire, approve, disapprove, or marvel at.

III. **Christ and St. Paul,** in the texts quoted, convey:

A. **A Tribute.** It is a glorious thing to be set up over the world to light, to guide, to warm, to be the city of refuge.

Note: Only the best are watched, scrutinized, used as models and guides.

B. **A Prophecy:** So the world has always treated Catholics; it watches, scrutinizes, observes, approves, disapproves:

1. *Their religion is never forgotten;* always and everywhere in business, politics, social life, etc., they are known to be Catholics.

Some unescapable character of Catholicism makes Catholics marked men, marked with the ineffaceable (though apparently invisible) mark of baptism.

12

2. *Their lives are scrutinized* to see how far their practice con-
forms with their faith and principles.
Only to Catholics is Christ's test continuously applied: "By
their fruits you shall know them."

3. The fact that *Catholics are quickly condemned* for defects
in conduct readily condoned in others indicates the good conduct expected of them.

This prophecy has been true throughout history:

1. Catholics and the Church are blamed for any abuses that happened during periods of Catholic influence; e.g., "The Dark Ages"
are attributed to the Church, though during them the Church,
which did not cause them, was actually curing them and bringing
men from barbarism into the civilization of modern Europe. On
the other hand, Protestantism is not blamed for the darkest of
modern eras, the early nineteenth-century industrial development
in England, though England was solidly Protestant. Catholics are
blamed for the Inquisition; Protestants are not blamed for the
Penal Laws of England and Ireland.

2. History repeats itself today. Every defect or mistake of Catholic
countries is referred to as Catholic; decay of morals or religion in
Protestant countries is not associated with Protestantism.

C. **A Warning:** If Catholics are a high city, a light, a spectacle,
the salt of the earth, they have:

1. *Responsibility:* Their lives must show forth the effects
of their principles. They must lead up to their high city,
not down to the mire. They must be a beacon, not an *ig-
nis fatuus*. They must preserve like salt, not destroy and
corrupt.

Note: Conversions to the Church are usually not by theory but by
example.

2. *Stewardship:* Catholics hold the fame and reputation of
the Catholic Church in their keeping.

Note 1: Saints are usually unknown to those outside the Church, except
the saints who were national figures. Few non-Catholics know devoted
priests, religious, or sisters. They know Catholic laymen and laywomen of
their own age and class. They judge the "living Church" by its living
representatives.

Note 2: The fact is clear that the observer is critical and severe and
often unjust in condemning Catholics for sins and faults not regarded as

important in others. This is because Catholics profess high standards of life, and *corruptio optimi, pessima,* "The best when corrupted become the worst."

IV. The Catholic college *student is not merely* **one of the followers** of Christ, but a trained, educated, intelligent follower of Christ:
   A. Attending Christ's *training school,* His West Point.
   B. With special *intellectual advantages* of which the world is aware.
   C. *Set aside* from others through education as well as religion.
   D. A self-confessed and *recognized leader.*

Hence, the Catholic college student in a special way:
   1. Is observed and watched — a spectacle.
   2. Is a light to those who look for guidance.
   3. Is the preservative of the world's morality and truth.

Inevitably this must bring a sense of responsibility, of privilege, of distinction.

V. **Exemplary conduct,** i.e., conduct that can serve as an example for others, the *shining example* is expected and demanded from the Catholic student.

Note: The college student, Catholic or non-Catholic, is directly and immediately associated with his school: "A senior from Blank College"; "A Freshman at Jones College." The Catholic college student is the representative in the eyes of observers of a Catholic college, not merely carrying before them its scholastic standards but its moral and religious standards as well.

VI. **The Shining Example shows itself:**
   A. *In speech,* the first manifestation of the content of mind and soul.

Quite aside from any question of right or wrong, sin or virtue, speech betrays the character, thought, habits, mental equipment, and background of the individual.
   1. *Scandal* inevitably follows *vulgarity or profanity* from a Catholic student, e.g., on the athletic field, in the dressing rooms, in the restaurant, or at a party.
   2. *Unclean talk* betrays the *filthy mind* and debased, animal tastes. To the observer it shows the interest of the Catholic student in sin and its fulfillment.
   3. *Taking sides with the enemies of the Church,* in conversation

and arguments and discussions, is treason. Catholics are expected instinctively by non-Catholics to defend the Church's position.

4. *On essential dogmas:* e.g., Papal infallibility; the fact of sin; free will; the unique commission Christ gave only to His Church.

5. *On things that regard conduct,* formerly regarded as essential by all decent men; now still held firmly by the Church: e.g., the evil of sexual laxity; the restless quest of a good time at all costs; birth control.

6. *On Catholic Practice:* knowing its meaning, importance, and value: e.g., Sunday Mass; fasting; Friday abstinence; Catholic devotions.

B. **In conduct:** Low standards of conduct regarded as not unusual in certain other groups, even collegiate groups, are a surprise, shock, and scandal in Catholic students.

Note: Conduct is either the external expression of principles or beliefs, or else it is treason against these principles.

1. *Moderation* in everything; e.g., in drinking. The Catholic Church has never opposed *drink* as evil in itself nor moderate drinking in those who are not harmed by it. But it emphatically insists on temperance for all and recommends total abstinence for young people:

a) Because it helps them train and form their character.

b) Because alcohol excites and stimulates the passions at a time of life when they are naturally strong.

c) Because it lowers moral resistance to temptation.

d) Because abstinence is an example to those who drink to excess.

e) Because it is a sacrifice made in union with Christ suffering from thirst upon the cross.

2. *Excessive drinking:*

a) Ruins health.

b) Corrupts morals and leads to immediate and violent temptations.

c) Weakens the will.

d) Destroys the ability to enjoy decent and worth-while pleasures.

      e) Seriously interferes with the ability to work or study.

      f) Forms habits that may do harm to an entire future.

Note: Few young people drink alone. Invariably they become the source of temptation to others. Contrast the scandal of a drunken college man (and the deeper scandal of a drunken college woman) with the strength and clear-headed self-control of a student who can refuse a drink, keep self-mastery, and hold himself in command.

   3. *Clean, pure conduct.* (The question of sexual purity, its value, motives, etc., will be treated in Chapter XXIII.) *Non-Catholics expect* purity of Catholic students:

      a) Because their *religion demands purity.*

      b) Because they come in contact with the *pure Eucharistic* Christ.

      c) Because of their attitude toward *Mary, Virgin and Mother.*

      d) Because they profess to regard *women as important* and respect them as virgins, nuns, wives, mothers.

      e) Because they *reverence family life.*

      f) Because they *reverence children.*

   4. *Scrupulous Honesty:* The highest tribute paid to a man by men of the world is, "He is scrupulously honest"; "His word is his bond"; "He can be trusted implicitly." The same tribute is paid to women. The most insulting charge is that of being a liar, a thief, untrustworthy, dishonorable.

Yet the constantly recurring charge against *college students* is that they are *dishonest:*

      a) *Regarding school:*

      (1) Cheating in examinations.

      (2) Copying one another's work.

      (3) Handing down and accepting book reports, laboratory notes.

      b) *Regarding home:*

      (1) Deceiving their parents, about "dates"; actual destinations; use of money.

      (2) Accepting a college education, and then neglecting its opportunities.

      (3) Actual taking of money and misusing it.

Whatever the charge, Catholic college students are expected to set high standards of external conduct. The judgment of the casual observer or the man of the world often is based solely upon this.

Problems and Discussions

1. Is the world unfair in demanding a higher standard of conduct from Catholics? Is it true that it does make such a demand?

2. Debate: It is a privilege and honor to be placed by God as a "spectacle" before the world.

3. What is (or was) the religion of Franklin D. Roosevelt, Alfred E. Smith, Babe Ruth, Charles Lindbergh, Max Schmeling, Helen Wills Moody, Ramon Navarro, Kathleen Norris, David I. Walsh, Bobby Jones, Gene Tunney, Owen D. Young, Mary Roberts Rinehart, Alfonso of Spain, Norma Shearer, Charles Schwab? From your answers could you argue that members of the Catholic Church alone, whatever their profession or repute, are always associated with their religion?

4. Is this a true or false statement: Scandals by outstanding Catholics are the greatest reason why the Catholic Church does not make more converts. Give reasons and examples to illustrate your decision.

5. If the test, "By their fruits ye shall know them" was applied to the students of your college, what would an impartial observer decide about the faith and principles of the student body?

6. Discuss the following statements:
    a) After all, youth must have its fling.
    b) She's a Catholic but she swears like a truck driver.
    c) I don't mind a dirty story if it's clever.
    d) He has the good old Catholic vice of drunkenness.
    e) She was tight as a hoot owl, and was she funny.
    f) The family thought I went to my cousin's; but I went to the Silver Slipper.

7. Answer the non-Catholic who says: "Since you come from a Catholic college, I expect better things from you than I do from the student of a state university."

8. Discuss this statement: "The example of good Catholics is the greatest influence for the conversion of the world."

9. How practically can the student be handled by his clean-minded associates when he persists in telling off-color stories?

10. What is the moral difference between vulgarity and obscenity in speech? Is there much difference in the eyes of the non-Catholic observing a Catholic in this connection?

11. Trace the story of the Church's attitude toward temperance and total abstinence.

12. Debate: The moral situation would be made less difficult for young men and young women, if the pledge of total abstinence while at school were adopted.

13. Analyze this statement: A young man who is careless in his treatment of young women disgraces his own mother and has low ideals of motherhood.

14. Analyze this statement: "I, a non-Catholic, visited a Catholic college, found the students dishonest in class, examinations, and assignments, and lost all interest in the Catholic religion."

Suggested Readings

PAMPHLETS

Loyola University Press:
His Last Retreat, Jottings of a College Freshman.

BOOKS

Lives of the Saints, at the choice of the professor.
Stoddard, *Rebuilding a Lost Faith* (Kenedy).
Williams, *The High Romance* (Macmillan).
Dudley, *The Masterful Monk* (Longmans).
Benson, *Religion of the Plain Man* (Burns & Oates).

Chapter IV

QUALITIES EXPECTED OF A CATHOLIC COLLEGE STUDENT OR ANY CATHOLIC LEADER

3. Use of Opportunities

Relatively a small percentage of modern men and women have the advantage of a college education. A much smaller proportion have the further privilege of a Catholic college education. Hence, those who do have this advantage and privilege have a responsibility for using it to the best advantage.

I. **College educations** are given for the **following purposes:**

    A. *Actually to learn definite facts,* criteria, standards of judgment, appreciation, proper valuation of self; all these to be used to make a success of life and to aid in gaining eternity.

    B. *To learn how to learn more* later on, since all life is a constant widening of horizon, increasing of knowledge, gathering of experience, etc.

    C. *To learn how to work,* so that through continued work, the individual may master a career and through it win success.

    D. *To establish social relationships* (called today contacts) so as to fit the individual better to take his place in society, the business world, organizations, the state, through a deeper knowledge of human nature and a highly developed power of working with others.

    E. In general, *to develop the individual* in a way that fits him for success in life and eternity.

II. **Two types of students face this education:**

    A. The student who regards *college as a pleasant four years of friendship, good times,* social life, athletics, and things of that type, interrupted by inevitable classes and lectures and laboratory periods.

    B. The student who realizes that *four years are given:*

    1. *To acquire important information* and to develop important mental operations, appreciations, standards.

2. *To acquire habits* that will insure success in life.
3. *To learn to do well* everything done, since the "art of doing things well" makes for later success.

Note: The apparently brilliant and successful and outstanding student at college may not necessarily be the successful individual later on in life:

1. He may have been clever and found it easy to learn; hence, he succeeded without learning to work.
2. He may have been "flashy," but flashes give little light and less heat.
3. He may, because of easy victories at school later fail when faced with the hard and merciless competitions and demands of life.

Hence: Notably successful alumni and alumnae are seldom from the top or the bottom of the class. They are usually the group that:

1. Used opportunities to develop their gifts whether large or small.
2. Learned to work, for work is essential for success in later life.

III. **In learning definite facts,** criteria, standards of judgment and appreciation, the student should remember the following:

   A. *No fact learned is ever wasted or lost,* no matter how apparently unimportant or unrelated to actual life it may seem.
   B. *From a clear knowledge of the past,* we judge the present and the future:
      1. Since *history* keeps repeating itself.
      2. *Literature* is judged by the masterpieces and the masters of the past.
      3. *Modern thought* becomes intelligible in the light of past thought.
      4. *Man's contemporaneous problems* are often solved in the light of similar problems in the past.
   C. *"When a man learns a new language,* he puts on a new soul" — whether he remembers the language later or not.
   D. *Standards of criticism* awaken a sound judgment that is a sure guide through life, whether this is criticism of books, objective truth, music, heroism, scientific values, or other things.
   E. *New scientific data* accumulate on the basis of old data and are intelligible only because of them.

IV. **All this is most valuable for oneself.**

    A. *An ignorant man is a dull and uninterested man. An educated* man is alert and alive, interesting and interested in everything. Each new fact or principle opens new fields and ideas for mental exploration:

        1. Through *books.*

        2. Through *current events.*

        3. Through *intelligent conversation.*

        4. Through the *arts.*

        5. Through contact with *scientific advances.*

    B. An educated man meets all men and women *on terms of equality,* joins organizations feeling that he has a right to belong, and is a leader not a follower.

    C. An educated man is *never bored* even when most alone. He finds companionship in books, music, scenery, the stars, thought, reflection.

    D. He is the *source of real pleasure* and satisfaction to others. He has things to say; knows what to do and how to do it; is a pleasant companion and a welcome guest.

Note: What is said of men is today notably true of women who, when educated, are the patrons of literature, the arts, drama, lectures, civic movements along cultural lines, and varied enterprises.

V. **In learning how to learn more later during life,** the student should remember the following:

    A. *Education closes only with death* when the Final Examination takes place. The years of college really:

        1. *Open avenues for later exploration,* e.g., through travel, reading, contact with various types of people, scientific study, concerts, general experience.

        2. Teach the means by which to *profit from later contacts,* give standards for judgment, correctness of viewpoint, bases for comparison, and actual methods and systems for studying and acquiring constantly increased knowledge.

        3. *Start habits of observation,* correct reading (contrasted with haphazard, desultory, quickly forgotten reading) scientific and historical accuracy, mastery of approach to source material, all of which can be used through life.

Note: Learning to learn is most important. Ignorant men see without learning, experience without profiting. Educated men are constantly learning from everything with which they come in contact.

VI. **In learning to work,** the following are important considerations.

A. Mankind knows from history and from recurrently bitter experience that *no success is achieved without work.*

B. "Genius is one part inspiration and ninety-nine parts perspiration."

C. Luck with work may bring success; but luck without work never brings lasting success.

    1. *In modern business,* where tense activity and intense competition make work, planning, thought essential.

    2. *In literature,* where no one ever finds writing easy.

    3. *In science,* where only tireless application brings results.

    4. *In professional life,* where accurate knowledge, medical or legal, must be supplemented by unremitting devotion to work.

    5. *In artistic lines,* where great painters, actors, musicians, work like slaves for their results.

    6. *In home life,* where successful mothers, wives, hostesses, plan and give thought and work to their careers.

Note: *Work is a habit that can be developed* and cultivated. *Four years of loafing* through college:

    1. *Often unfit a person for work* later on when work is essential. Clever intellectual tramps fill the world with their inaptitude.

    2. Often *persuade* a person *that work is not really necessary* for success.

    3. *Create habits of indolence* and slovenliness and inaccuracy that mark them for later failures.

The few examples of later successes who apparently loafed through college are often quoted. Usually in their apparent loafing they were working hard at the thing they afterwards used for success, writing, painting, music, science. They are the rare exceptions who only prove the rule.

The establishment of social relationships is treated in Chapter VI.

VII. Does this emphasis on work imply there is to be little social life?

    • On the contrary, regular and sane social life is an aid to success in college studies, and will aid in later life. But it does imply *a decent devotion to the main purposes of college:*

    A. *In Class:* Class may be wasted (used for sleep, reading, correspondence, other work) or used to advantage:

        1. *To gain real knowledge.*

2. *To learn concentration.*

3. *To save oneself time* outside of class. A student who follows the professor will be spared much cramming later on — notably at examination time.

Note: The professor or instructor is an expert giving the net results of his studies and training. Even when dull in presentation, his facts and conclusions are important.

a) **A notebook** well kept in class:

(1) Gets down the best and *most important data.*

(2) Prevents the *untrustworthy memory* from being burdened.

(3) Keeps the *mind alert.*

b) *Outside of class:*

(1) *Day-by-day study* as compared with cramming means:

(*a*) *Material learned and remembered,* where crammed material is immediately forgotten.

(*b*) *Facts and conclusions made a permanent part* of the mental equipment, not a mere surface contact immediately lost.

(2) Briefly, an easy method of study is this:

(*a*) *Review briefly, as soon after class* as possible, the material in the notebook.

(*b*) *Reread these notes* the following day before class.

(*c*) *Go through the text* while the professor's explanation is still fresh.

(*d*) *Review the whole week's work* briefly once a week.

(*e*) **Results:** Enormous amount of time saved, and the knowledge gained is retained permanently.

Note: It is important to learn to lean on one's own abilities and not on the abilities of others. Material taken from others, either in the traditionally handed-down notes or in copied material, is valueless except for the report mark. It means nothing in permanent mental equipment or value for life. What one learns for oneself:

1. Is remembered.

2. Is part of one's mental equipment.

3. Has trained the mind.

4. And strengthened the will.

Marks are no indication of what has been permanently gained from the course. The important questions in the course are:

    1. Whether the material of the course has been mastered.

    2. Whether from the course the student has learned to learn.

    3. Whether because of it, he knows a little more about how to master a difficult job.

VIII. **The Catholic college student is not living a Catholic life but merely learning external facts, unless he supernaturalizes his work:**

    A. He can make of this work a direct service of God and through it win real merit for himself:

        1. By use of the morning offering.

        2. By brief visits to the Blessed Sacrament during the day.

        3. By attentive prayer before and after class.

        4. By trying to realize that he offers up his work in union with:

            a) Jesus in the carpenter shop.

            b) Mary and Joseph in their work.

            c) The Church Militant throughout the world.

        5. By remembering that the four years of training will make him the type of Catholic leader for whom the Catholic Church and the world is hoping.

Problems and Discussions

1. Compare the inaccurate opinions of the average self-educated man with the accurate statements and standards of judgment of a well-educated college man.

2. What would you as a parent expect college to do for the training of a son or a daughter? What would you expect a son or a daughter to get from it?

3. Discuss the correctness or incorrectness of this statement: "The most valuable thing a student gets from college is social contacts."

4. Criticize the following statement: "Only fools work."

5. List a series of notable men and women to show they achieved success by working; by sheer luck without work.

6. Tell a young man (or woman) what he should expect to get from a scientific course; a literary course; a history course.

7. What is the meaning of the statement: "A man who learns a new language puts on a new soul"?

8. Why is it important to learn to learn?

9. Describe "an intellectual tramp."

10. Take any one of your freshmen courses and show how it can be used to fulfill the purposes of a college training.

11. Discuss the following statements:

    a) "I don't need to study; I can plug up all the matter the night before examination."

    b) "Only drudges take notes in class."

    c) "I sleep through Professor Blank's class; he's too dead to keep me awake."

    d) "All you need is just to get by."

    e) "I borrowed a grand set of notes from a sophomore who took the course last year."

    f) "A set of ponies is going to carry me through this year's work."

12. What is meant by "broadening your horizon"?

13. Why is it important nowadays to know how to work? Can college really teach this?

14. What is the precise value of supernaturalizing one's work at college? How can it be done effectively?

Suggested Readings

Note: For the next three chapters the Reading List can be gone over and assigned readings designated for the student.

To supplement these three chapters:

PAMPHLETS

The Queen's Work Press:
Our Precious Freedom, Lord, S.J.
Why Leave Home, Lord, S.J.
Hours Off, Lord, S.J.
The Ruling Passion, Lord, S.J.

BOOKS

Lindworsky, *The Training of the Will* (Bruce).
Hull, *Formation of Character* (Herder; Kenedy).
Helps to Self-Knowledge (America Press).

Chapter V

QUALITIES EXPECTED OF A CATHOLIC COLLEGE STUDENT OR ANY CATHOLIC LEADER

4. Honor and Honesty

I. **Honor and honesty** in times past have been praised as typical of all high-minded men, pagan as well as Christian. High commendation was contained in such statements as these:

His word is his bond.

His word is as binding as his oath.

In his conduct, he is absolutely trustworthy.

He is in everything scrupulously honest.

He touches nothing to which he has not a clear right.

He would rather be right than president.

In similar relationships, these are true praises of women. *Youth's insistence* has made the world believe it considered itself **peculiarly and distinctively honest.** "Other generations may have other virtues; the present generation is honest," is a proud boast and an important one

Note: *Frankness and honesty are not the same.* Frankness is merely the plain admission of qualities, bad as well as good; an inclination to speak truth regarding oneself. But a gangster, thoroughly dishonest, may be frank and almost boastful about his criminal conduct. A student, dishonest in dealing with parents, may be frank about this dishonesty in talking with fellow students.

II. **Honor and honesty** are developed and reasonable trustworthiness of conduct, mental attitude, speech are aided by recalling the universally accepted principles that:

   A. Dishonesty in *any form is theft,* made cowardly and cheap because usually involving a victim unable to defend himself.

   B. Dishonor is a kind of *spiritual suicide,* meriting a complete or partial loss of respect in the eyes of fellow men.

   C. Dishonesty *takes advantage of another's weakness,* often when the other trusts implicitly.

   D. Dishonor and dishonesty deservedly cost a man or woman *the loss of the confidence* of fellow men.

26

III. **Honor and honesty** in a Catholic college student have these additional *motives:*

    A. *Christ,* the model of manhood, was the soul of honor and honesty.

    B. The student while realizing the importance of supernatural virtues, *will not allow pagans to excel* in natural virtues.

    C. Dishonesty is *almost always connected with sin,* often serious.

    D. He knows that, if he is not trustworthy at college, he will *not be trustworthy later on in life;* for honor and honesty are habits, developed through practice.

    E. Dishonesty, however slight, is a *blight on character.*

IV. **Honor and honesty in class** consist in claiming credit only for the knowledge actually possessed and for work actually done.

Any mark in studies above what is actually merited by work and knowledge (unless the element of luck enters in), if gained unlawfully is a form of trickery.

Note: College students admit (and almost seem to boast) of the existence of a surprising amount of cheating. Cheating takes by underhand means the knowledge and work of another. It is an implicit misstatement to the instructor and the class and is in all forms dishonest.

V. **Honesty in college:**

    A. **In examinations:**

        1. Copying in examination is the taking of marks to which one is not entitled no matter what form the copying takes, e.g., from notes, from the papers of others, from the hidden text, etc.

        a) It puts the honest student to a great disadvantage; his marks may actually suffer in comparison with the student who cheats.

        b) It harms the cheater:

        (1) His paper is a written and untrue claim to know facts he actually does not know.

        (2) He has learned to *substitute dishonesty* for work.

        (3) He has actually been deceitful and tricky, an action which leaves its effects on the soul and the character.

        c) It misleads the professor:

        (1) Who gets a false impression of the standing of his class.

        (2) Who does not know what has really been learned from his course.

(3) Whose teaching is thereby impaired, harming both the honest students and the cheaters.

B. *Copying the work of another,* even when the other is willing, is the act of a parasite, in addition to the other things true of cheating in examination. This applies to copying in examination, book reports, experiments, translations, taking themes done by someone else, etc. Through copying:

1. The student *loses all the advantages* of actual study.
2. He really *learns little,* and what he learns is almost immediately forgotten.
3. He gets in the *habit of weakly leaning on another.*
4. He is a *mental pickpocket,* picking his classmates' brains.
5. He develops: *A weak will;* laziness, a habit of depending on someone else, an inability to master a difficulty.
6. He often gets *false values* to the extent of despising real students.

VI. **Cheating** clearly manifests vices already existing:

A. *Cowardice:* The student is afraid to accept before parents, professors, friends, the just consequences of his own usually culpable ignorance and laziness.

B. *Hypocrisy:* He desires to appear better than he really is.

VII. **College Rules** are given:

A. On the supposition that, while college students may be adults or at least developing adults, experienced men and women will be able best *to guide them* during their important years.

B. Because rules are *necessary* to secure:

1. *Satisfactory work* and satisfactory results from class and courses.
2. Moral and physical *security* for the students who are for the time "the family" of the college.
3. A *training* in rule-observance necessary:
   a) For good citizenship. A state without laws would be an anarchy.
   b) For success in business. All businesses today have strict and carefully enforced rules.
   c) For training in leadership. No leader is safe in giving his commands if he has not learned to obey the commands of others.

VIII. Honesty at Home:

This is primarily concerned with conduct *toward parents or guardians.*

A. As long as a son or daughter lives under the paternal roof and accepts the paternal support, he is bound by the wishes and rules of the parents.

Note: When a student pays his own way through college, his work or lack of it in college may be his own concern. When he accepts a college education from his parents, he implicitly accepts a responsibility to use this opportunity as well as he can.

B. Hence, it is *dishonorable and dishonest:*

1. *To deceive parents,* e.g., about the student's whereabouts, destination when leaving for a party or week-end, about the use of one's evenings, about friends, amusements, associations, etc.

2. *To accept the benefits,* comforts, and luxuries of the home and deliberately to disobey the wishes and rules of those who provide them.

3. To accept from parents a college education and then *squander these opportunities* by loafing, failing to study, getting low grades through one's own fault, using it merely as a chance for a good time.

Note: A son and daughter will do well to measure their conduct toward parents on the basis of what later they will expect from their own children for whom they will make sacrifices.

C. *Honesty toward brothers and sisters* implies:

1. A decent respect for their rights and property, no matter how young or small the brother or sister may be:

   a) No taking without permission.

   b) No borrowing without permission.

   c) No intrusion upon their mail, telephone calls, personal friendships.

IX. Honor and Honesty among Equals:

A. **Sincerity** is merely another form of honesty. Sincerity expresses itself in speech, in conduct: the saying and doing of things which one really means. Insincerity is the expression through words of conduct of thoughts and emotions one does not feel and is distinctly dishonorable.

    1. *Lies* hardly need discussion. They are cheap, tricky, the height of insincerity, taking advantage of another's guileless ignorance.

Note: No worse insult can be leveled at a man or woman than the name, Liar!

    2. *Insincerity*, strictly so called. Flattery of another or the expression of a deep interest really not felt (the use of a "line") for personal profit or gain is cheap and dishonorable; e.g., a girl showing exaggerated interest in or affection for a young man simply because he can give her a good time; a boy giving a girl attention or affection that he does not mean, simply because he does this with every attractive girl.

B. **Respect for the rights of others.**

    1. *Their good name.* Even when serious sin is not involved, gossip, scandal, repetition of stories that harm character or spoil friendships are dishonorable and dishonest.

    2. *Their personal property.*

      a) Taking another's things with presumed permission, borrowing clothes, sporting goods, books, unread magazines, etc., is often very close to theft, and always most annoying.

      b) Taking another's things with permission is usually a great inconvenience. Borrowing in any form except under strict necessity is an almost certain way of spoiling friendships.

      (1) Borrowed articles can seldom be replaced.

      (2) Decent people hardly know how to refuse a borrower.

      (3) Borrowed articles are returned in less satisfactory condition, especially clothes, sporting goods, books.

      (4) A borrower is a parasite and a pest and universally disliked and avoided.

X. **Honor and Honesty in smaller details** expresses itself:

A. In acknowledging invitations promptly and courteously. Unanswered invitations cause the host and hostess annoyance, leave them uncertain about the number of guests, often result in useless expense, and indicate bad breeding on the part of the invited guest.

B. *In expressing prompt gratitude for gifts.* The sender meant the gift to cause pleasure; it probably involved some expense on his part. If the gift is not acknowledged, he does not know whether it has been received, pleased the receiver, or was lost. A gift demands adequate expression of gratitude.

C. *In touching nothing* to which one has no right, e.g., fruit in stores, magazines on stands, candy on counters, etc.

D. *In paying just fines;* e.g., to library for overdrawn books, to club for late dues, etc.

Note: Important is the accusation made against college students that many of them "beat" tradespeople out of small bills, and sometimes larger ones:

1. Delaying payment when they can afford to pay.
2. Avoiding payment altogether for no just reason.
3. Running up bills they cannot afford to pay. This is a form of theft, may be serious matter for a mortal sin, and brings disgrace and disrepute on the college whose students, even a few of them, practice it.

XI. **Personal honor** (integrity of character, truthfulness, straightforwardness, strict honesty) is:

A. One of the highest of the *natural virtues.*

B. A virtue that makes a man or woman admired and attractive.

C. A virtue that is *developed through years of practice.*

D. And *sacrificed by slight and continuous faults* against honor and honesty.

On the contrary *a dishonorable person is despised* and universally regarded with suspicion:

A liar is regarded as beneath contempt.

An untrustworthy person lives under constant suspicion.

Dishonor is prelude to social and business death.

An honorable man or woman whose word is accepted and whose speech and conduct are beyond suspicion walks:

1. Fearless of consequences of dishonorable conduct.
2. Respected by right-minded men and women as certain and trustworthy.
3. Conscious of his strength and self-mastery.

Problems and Discussions

1. Give instances from pagan history of respect for one's word of honor. Of high regard for truth and honesty.
2. Could you describe in fuller detail a man of whom it is said: "His word is his bond"?
3. What makes the term "liar" so fearful an insult?

4. Even if a student failed in an examination, would you consider it true that honesty is the best policy? Give reasons for your answer.

5. Discuss the following statements with a view to honor and honesty:
   a) I do half the experiments; J does the other half; and then we swap.
   b) I told the dean I was going to my aunt's for dinner, and then slipped down to town instead.
   c) What Dad and Mother don't know won't worry them.
   d) Mary's a pretty good girl, but she hands all men the same line.

6. Is there a moral or ethical problem involved in the following? J copies in an important examination and thereby wins the sophomore English medal and $20 in gold. T, who did not cheat, came second by half a point.

7. Discuss the statement: A student who uses another student's biology experiment book is a parasite.

8. While B does not copy, he writes the themes for three other men in English composition class. Discuss.

9. A parent stints himself to send a son (or daughter) through college. The student who has considerable ability in English, wastes his time reading cheap magazines in class. What of honor or honesty is involved?

10. Define and illustrate the words *trustworthy, sincerity*.

11. Discuss with a view to honor and honesty the student who runs up bills at the local drug store which he knows he is not likely to be able to pay?

12. A student consistently borrows the clothes of a roommate, sometimes with, sometimes without permission. What is to be said of this conduct?

13. An older brother consistently takes without permission the golf balls of a younger brother "because it's all in the family." What of this conduct?

14. When a question of religion comes up J says nothing in defense of the Church simply because he does not want to make possible enemies. Discuss.

15. A student is very sweet and gracious to a teacher while in that teacher's class simply to be able to make better marks.

Chapter VI

QUALITIES EXPECTED OF A CATHOLIC COLLEGE STUDENT OR ANY CATHOLIC LEADER

5. Comradeship

I. **The social life** of a college student is most important, for;
   A. During college days the student is expected:
      1. *To establish social contacts* with students of like taste and characteristics and general attitudes toward life.
      2. *To form friendship* for the time of college and for life.
      3. *To develop the human instinct for organization.*
   B. Man is a highly "social animal"; that is, he tends by nature to associate with and join with his fellow men. (This is explained fully in Ethics.) Briefly:
      1. *He needs the society* of his fellows.
      2. *He forms organizations* to help himself and others.
      3. *He develops best* when surrounded by sympathetic, congenial, stimulating, and inspiring people.
   C. Hence, the importance of the fact that at college:
      1. Varieties of young men and women meet both as individuals and as members of organizations.
      2. Have the chance to associate, develop, and establish contacts and friendships, and to work and play under favorable conditions.

II. **These personal contacts** are valuable:
   A. **For the actual years of college:**
      1. Every student comes to know the pleasures of congenial companionship in working, playing, associating with students engaged in the same general pursuits as himself. The fact that these come from different walks of life, often from different sections of the country, makes this contact varied and delightful.
   B. **For life.**
      1. Associations of school must stand the test of life, not of just the immediate present. College friendships are best when they are likely to endure into full adult life.

III. **The social instincts** of a Catholic college student should manifest these qualities:

  A. *Breadth of interest.* A wise student will get to know many of his fellows with as many varied abilities and tastes as possible.

    1. **Cliques** *are uniformly bad:*

     a) For the school. They put group spirit ahead of school spirit, substitute club for college, and destroy the unity of the student body.

     b) For the individual.

      (1) They deprive him or her of those who might be the most valuable associates. One who belongs to a clique seldom knows others outside that group; those outside the group seldom care to know those in the group.

      (2) They throw him with groups of individuals too like himself in interests, training, background, and consequently eliminate those whose differences would prove stimulating and interesting.

      (3) They create the general impression of snobbishness that brings about a complete lack of sympathy with the great student body.

     c) Breadth of interest, on the contrary, introduces the student to those of:

      (1) Varied backgrounds.

      (2) Varied tastes and interests.

      (3) And trains the student to meet varieties of people in later life.

  B. *Generosity.*

    1. Best friendships are usually connected not with a person who has been generous to us, but with the person to whom we have been generous. To form and cement friendships, generosity is essential:

     a) A genuine willingness to help — especially the newcomer, the slightly shy student, the student with difficulties in special subjects, the foreigner.

     b) A willingness to share — especially one's friends, books, knowledge, special privileges.

     c) A willingness to listen. The person who makes the most and best friends is not the good talker but the good listener.

Most people are lonely at least at times; the student ready to give a willing ear, is the student who wins friends, confidences, trust.

    d) A spirit of give-and-take. If inclined to joke, the student will be willing to take a joke; if asking favors will grant them; if accepting hospitality (large or small) will return it.

    e) An ability to inspire trust. This means:

      (1) *Keeping implicitly any secret* intrusted by a friend. One who cannot keep a confidence does not deserve it and soon will not get it.

      (2) *Avoiding gossip.* This is the curse of much college life which:

        (*a*) Separates friends.

        (*b*) Destroys characters.

        (*c*) Is usually untrue and based on lies.

        (*d*) Is often seriously sinful.

Note: A serious mortal sin of gossip is committed when the serious secret sin of a person is told to someone who has no right to know it.

    f) Combined with all this, however, must be a realization that *personal loyalty and friendship must not* come before:

      (1) *The good of the whole student body.*

      (2) *The good of the majority.*

      (3) *The good name of the school.*

For example, false loyalty keeps from the ears of the proper authorities grave wrongs (sins that harm others) that should be reported in order to save endangered victims or the reputation of the college. It is always wise to consult a confessor in a case of this kind.

IV. College organizations offer:

    A. *Training in group action.*

    B. *Special opportunities* for association along specialized lines.

    C. *A spirit of coöperation* and sympathetic understanding.

    D. Social and athletic and scholastic *possibilities.*

Note: At this point a brief survey of the chief organizations of the college may be in place.

    E. *Organizations should develop:*

    1. *Leadership* and an expert grasp on problems.

    2. *A feeling of fellowship,* and closer friendships.

3. *The spirit of coöperation* without which success in later life is very difficult.

4. *Increased strength* through union with congenial people working along the same lines.

V. **Social life** is important and a recognized part of Catholic college life. It should offer the student:

A. *Real relaxation.* Social life should refresh, give the student more energy and zest for his work, rebuild, and be generally wholesome.

B. *Contact with people* whom he finds refreshing and stimulating according to the standards of educated men.

C. *A type approved by the college.* Official social life should be under college auspices and with faculty approval.

D. *Nothing that is wrong* or harmful or the cause of possible scandal to right-minded people.

E. Social life should be:

1. *Not too expensive* or elaborate.

   a) Few students can really afford it.

   b) Elaborate parties are usually tiresome and dull and too complicated for comfort or real contact.

   c) They set a standard difficult to maintain later on.

2. *Often on the college grounds:*

   a) Where students should play as well as work.

   b) Where the student meets his own kind.

   c) Where expenses can be curtailed, the spirit regulated, and the standard of good taste kept high.

VI. Back of Catholic comradeship are **these supernatural ideals:**

A. Catholic students are *all children of the same Father,* God.

B. They are *children of the same Mother,* Mary.

C. They are members of the *same Holy Mother Church.*

D. They are *brothers and sisters of Jesus Christ.*

E. Their *interests are united* through their common faith and philosophy and hope of eternal life to be spent together.

Problems and Discussions

1. Discuss the following types of students:

   a) He (or she) goes entirely with the fellow students from his home town.

    b) He (or she) enters college determined to meet as many types of students as possible.

    c) He (or she) refuses to join any organizations.

    d) He (or she) joins them all.

2. Is it possible for a student to have a few intimate friends and yet associate with a great many others? Is this wise or not?

3. Discuss the student who develops most of his social contacts outside of college.

4. Describe a typical clique and its effect upon the whole spirit of the school.

5. What are the qualities that make for real comradeship?

6. Analyze this statement: The best friend is not one who talks best but one who listens best.

7. Criticize the following statements:

    a) Gossip is inevitable at school and merely entertaining.

    b) Students can be loyal only to those of their own sex.

    c) No one has a right to tell a secret if he doesn't want it repeated.

    d) J is leading a group of younger men into sin, but I'm not a "stool pigeon" and I won't tell the dean.

8. What organizations do you think essential for a college?

9. What qualities in a student inspire the trust and confidence of other students?

10. Debate: Most college social life should be on the campus.

11. What type of friendships are likely to endure through later life?

12. What does this expression mean to you: The brotherhood of Christ?

13. Discuss this statement: To work with thoroughly uncongenial people is a magnificent training for later life.

Chapter VII

THE CHAPEL

I. It is characteristic of **a Catholic College to center around the chapel.** The chapel is sometimes called the heart of the college. In it regular services are conducted, sometimes of obligation, sometimes of invitation. Its importance in the student's life must make the chapel deeply significant.

II. Practically **all universities** and colleges whether Catholic or not **retain the chapel:**
   A. Because universities were established during Catholic times when chapels were significant.
   B. *However,* the chapel in all except Catholic colleges are:
      1. Empty of the "Presence," of the Blessed Sacrament which is the real living presence of Christ, the Son of God, remaining with His friends.
      2. Merely meeting places for worship. The early name for Protestant chapels and churches was "meeting house." In many of them the "worship" must be made purely an ethical talk, or some prayer sufficiently indefinite to displease none of the religions represented.
   C. Catholic chapels very different:
      1. They are built for the living presence of God.
      2. They are houses of definite faith, definite prayer, forms of worship ancient and important and effective.

III. The **Catholic college chapel** is usually filled with objects of historical significance:
   A. *The Altar.* The central act of worship is sacrifice which requires an altar. The chapel altar connects directly:
      1. With the altars of the Old Law.
      2. The Paschal Supper Table of the Last Supper when Christ celebrated the last Paschal sacrifice and instituted the new sacrifice of the New Law.
      3. The altars in the catacombs, which were the tombs of the martyrs.

4. The altars from the first century down through the centuries.

B. *The Stations,* which recall the Passion, the Holy Land, the pilgrimages made by the Christian world to the Tomb of the Savior.

C. *The Statues,* which suggest the Communion of Saints, the Church Triumphant, and our historic heroes and heroines.

D. *The Altar and Shrine of Mary:*
  1. Seat of Wisdom.
  2. Instructress of the Boy Christ.
  3. Mother of the Catholic student.

E. *The Altar of St. Joseph,* reminding the student of the value of simple work.

IV. **Architecturally** the chapel usually contains *a summary of the story of the development* and progress of the Catholic Church:
  A. The altar recalls the *Catacombs.*
  B. The first floor plan was that of the *Roman law courts,* turned over by Constantine to the Christians: in the apse sat the Roman Judge; the clients were in the nave; the lawyers gathered around the columns.
  C. The change and development in the arches trace *the development of modern Europe,* from Roman to Romanesque; through Greek influence to Byzantine; through the barbarians civilized by the Church to Gothic; through the revival of the classic learning to the Renaissance.

V. **The Catholic college chapel is significant** because:
  A. *Christ, son of God, lives there in our midst:*
  1. *As a friend* accepting the hospitality of His friends. God is the best beloved guest; Christ is the honored "alumnus" of every Catholic college.
  2. *As a consultant* to those training to be His followers.
    a) If Christ could turn fishermen into Evangelists; as John the fisherman became the writer of the Fourth Gospel, the magnificent Epistles and the Apocalypse —
    b) If He could turn ignorant men like Peter and Matthew into fearless champions of truth —
    c) If He was the chief Teacher of all the saints: Augustine, learning through prayer; Bonaventure, using a crucifix as his text; Aquinas, almost dull till inspired by Christ —

d) If He is "the word of God," uncreated Wisdom, then the Catholic college student can take to Christ in the chapel, prayerfully, thoughtfully:

(1) His life problems.
(2) His personal difficulties.
(3) His problem of study and class.
(4) His future career.

Note: This can be done easily:

(*a*) Before the class day.
(*b*) During intervals or recesses.
(*c*) At the day's end.

3. *As a beloved Elder Brother,* who has experienced all our problems and difficulties and eagerly shows us the way:

a) *Through temptations:* He experienced three great temptations.

b) *Through misunderstandings:* He experienced them from His Apostles, friends, contemporaries, the great world.

c) *Through poverty:* He felt poverty as no student ever can.

d) *Through the sense of failure:* The Cross ended His career.

4. *As our Leader.* Christ is the world's only trustworthy and sure leader. He is keenly interested in college students and their progress, since they are His future Apostles to the world.

a) He approves their victories and successes.

b) He understands and sympathizes with their failures and defeats.

c) He guarantees complete victory in the end, no matter what the apparent failures and collapses of life.

(This will be more fully developed later.)

Note: This element of Christ's presence is the essential characteristic differentiating Catholic college chapels from:

1. Protestant churches.
2. Mosques or synagogues.
3. Even the most beautiful chapels of non-Catholic colleges or universities.

VI. **Chapel Service** is not a meaningless routine of school discipline, nor, as in many colleges, a survival of religious service the real meaning of which is gone. But it is:

A. *A review by the Leader* of his young followers. His future Catholic leaders present themselves to Christ, their Leader.

B. *A group prayer,* much more effective than solitary prayers:
Because:

  1. "Where two or three are gathered together in My name,
there am I in the midst of them."
Hence Christ is present in a special way with these college
groups.

  2. All unite in a common worship and a common need with
consequently added strength and mutual support.

C. *The time for counsel and direction* by one of God's representatives. (This will be treated more completely in Chapter XXV,
"Priestly Consultation.")

D. *Special and beautiful honor* is given to God and His Saints:

  1. Through the *Mass.*

  2. Through *Benediction:* Kneeling for the blessing of Christ
on lives and work.

  3. Through *Sacred Heart Devotion:* Reparation by youth for
the sins and blasphemies and disbeliefs of youth, and the
consecration of lives to the cause of Christ.

  4. Through Blessed Virgin devotions:

    a) Honor paid to Our Mother.

    b) Assistance begged from our powerful Mediatrix.

  5. Through special *devotions to the saints;* devotions which
are "memorial services" of living personalities strong enough
to help us effectively.

  6. Through the opportunity of offering up to God:

    a) The tedium of class.

    b) The observance of college regulations.

    c) The successes and defeats of the week.

VII. Hence, the **attitude of a Catholic college student** toward chapel
service should be that it is:

A. Not a burden but *an opportunity and a privilege.*

B. To be *used intelligently* not mechanically.

C. To be *planned by the individual himself,* who comes to the
service responsive, attentive, active, and not inert, relaxed,
passive.

VIII. **Voluntary Use of the Chapel** is as important as group use.

A. The college chapel is a twenty-four-hour-a-day chapel, open
for constant use.

B. **Visits** to the chapel bring:

1. *Strength against temptation* — from contact with the strength of Christ.
2. *Inspiration for our studies* — prayer is most important in mastering our subjects.
3. *The grace to take successes* without being spoiled by them — a difficult art and one not easy to learn.
4. *The grace to accept failures* bravely and to profit by them.
5. Visits may be:
    a) *Frequent,* whenever free time permits or class schedules allow.

Note: An excellent rule is never to pass a church or chapel without a call.

  b) *Brief,* for young men and young women move rapidly, and God understands this. If a long visit is difficult and discouragingly distracted, the call may be short and correspondingly earnest.
  c) *Purposeful.* The call should have a purpose in view and should be given a second's thought before it begins. The student may, for example:
   (1) Thank God for something.
   (2) Ask Him for something.
   (3) Mention some temptation.
   (4) Promise Him something.
   (5) Tell Him simply, as a child would tell a Father, that he loves Him.
   (6) Reconsecrate his loyalty to his Leader.

Problems and Discussions

1. Debate: In a Catholic college some compulsory chapel service is inevitable and wise.
2. Why, in view of the character of the chapel, do students in non-Catholic universities and colleges occasionally appear to rebel at compulsory chapel service?
3. What style of architecture is your college chapel? Compare it with your parish church. From what period of history did it arise? Trace its historical associations.
4. Criticize this statement: The chapel of a non-Catholic college is often a beautiful building stripped or emptied of its meaning.
5. Is this a good descriptive definition: "The chapel is the heart of the Catholic college"?
6. How did the Stations of the Cross originate?

7. Explain to a non-Catholic why Catholic chapels are open all the time.
8. What regular services would you suggest as proper for a Catholic college chapel?
9. Discuss these statements:
    a) J is so often in the chapel that he (or she) must be going to be a priest (or religious).
    b) A good gymnasium is more important to a Catholic college than a chapel.
    c) A daily visit to the chapel should be an accepted part of every college student's life.
    d) I don't like chapel services because the priest's talks are dull; I am distracted; the singing is terrible.
10. If you were taking a non-Catholic through your college chapel, how could you show him the significance, importance, and value of the chapel?
11. Discuss the following descriptive definitions of the chapel:
    a) It is God's consultation office.
    b) It is the oasis to life's traveler.
    c) The chapel is the Holy Land of the modern apostle.
12. What are some of the things that could be done during a brief voluntary visit to the chapel?

Suggested Readings

PAMPHLETS

Catholic Truth Society:
What You See in a Catholic Church, Martindale, S.J.

BOOKS

Cram, *The Catholic Church and Art* (Calvert Series) (Macmillan).
Betten, *The A B C of Church Architecture* (Bruce).
O'Hagan, *The Genesis of Christian Art* (Macmillan).

Chapter VIII

MASS — I

I. **The principal action** occurring within the college chapel is **the Celebration of Mass,** the offering up of the Holy Sacrifice.

   A. **For this the whole chapel is designed,** so much so that a chapel in which Mass is not said is purposeless and without object.

   1. *The altar* has for its only possible purpose the offering of sacrifice.

     a) When the Protestant Revolution abolished the Mass, it immediately destroyed the altar, leaving without meaning:

   2. *The apse* which was built to accommodate the altar.

   3. *All the lines* of the church or chapel which lead up to the altar, and the arches which bend above it.

II. **All the great religions,** until Protestantism, centered about sacrifice.

   A. **Sacrifice** in general is the offering of a gift to God as a sign of love, dependence, and the desire to serve Him.

   1. *Love inevitably shows itself in gifts:*

     a) Men give to the women they love.

     b) Parents give to children.

     c) "Say it with flowers" is the motto which means that gifts speak decisively of affection.

     d) Love is sealed with the gift of rings.

     e) Human instinct prompts the keeping of even the cheapest gifts because they are the indication of love on the part of the giver.

     f) *So a sacrifice is man's gift to God.*

   2. *Usually it is destroyed:*

     a) As a sign that *no one else, no human being, has any right to it ;* and since it has been given to God it is killed or burned so that it will be His alone.

     b) Because *God's authority over life is indicated* by the offering up of life — of animals, birds, etc.

     c) Because gifts offered to God *stand in place of the man* or

44

woman who offers the gift, and destruction indicates the willingness of the man to live or die at God's command.

III. Since sacrifice cannot have more than a certain number of types, it recurs throughout history in similar forms.

    A. **Throughout the old law:**

      1. *In pagan religions* (in which man's natural religious instincts expressed themselves, though often perverted and mistaken) sacrifices showed themselves:

        a) *In the offering of grain,* wine, the first fruits of the harvest, burned or presented in procession to God or the gods as a gift.

        b) *In the sacrificial killing of animals:*

          (1) Sometimes burned completely so that no human being could touch them.

          (2) Sometimes consumed and eaten in sacred banquets in honor of the gods.

        c) *In occasional human sacrifices.* This was the mistaken effort to give God or the gods the highest possible gift, human lives.

    B. *In the Jewish religion:*

      1. By God's express and definite appointment, complete *series of gifts* were to be offered Him:

        a) *Grains and fruits* from the harvests. Some of this was made into the Loaves of Proposition dedicated to the Temple.

        b) *Bread and wine,* as in the sacrifice of Melchisedech.

        c) *Animals.* Doves, lambs, oxen, goats, were the chief types. The flawless and perfect were given to God.

        d) *Human beings.* Each first-born son was offered to God in the temple, and then a lamb or dove was sacrificed "in his place." The young man's life was thus considered consecrated as a gift to God.

        e) *The Paschal Supper and banquet.* In this the lamb was eaten by the Jews as a sacred offering to God.

IV. Hence, **Sacrifice** is:

    A. **A natural expression of man's religious instinct,** and an expression approved and consecrated by God. It:

      1. *Gives God man's best,* in acknowledgment of God's supremacy.

2. *Shows God's dominion over life,* to indicate this supreme dominion over all things.

3. Through the symbolic offering of an animal, a man's possessions, the "first fruits" of his fields and herds, *it suggests and substitutes for the offering of the man himself to God.* And indicates man's dependence.

B. This instinct is *approved and commanded by God* in the Old Law.

Note: The Old Law foreshadowed the New; its heroes and prophets and kings "prefigured" the hero of the New Law, Jesus Christ. Hence, the sacrifices, so important in the Old Law, prefigured as sacrifice to begin with the New Law and be perfect.

C. *Practically all religions have had sacrifice* as an essential act of worship. Christ's own religion could not be:

1. Less natural in its satisfaction of man's instincts than the religions before His day.

2. Less perfect, omitting this important act of worship.

V. **The great sacrifice** of the New Law was **foretold and prefigured:**

A. The end of the sacrifices of the Old Law and the beginning of the new sacrifice is foretold *by the prophet Malachias,* I, 10,11.

"Who is there among you that will shut the doors and will kindle the fire on my altar gratis? I have no pleasure in you, saith the Lord of hosts: and I will not receive a gift of your hand.

"For from the rising of the sun even to the going down, My name is great among the Gentiles, and in every place there is sacrifice, and there is offered to My name a clean oblation; for My name is great among the Gentiles, saith the Lord of hosts."

B. *Of Christ* is it foretold by the inspired Psalmist:

"*Thou art a priest forever* according to the order of Melchisedech" Ps. 109, 4; referred to by St. Paul, Hebrews, V, 5.

C. *The sacrifices of the Old Law must have their fulfillment in the new.*

1. This was *predicted by Isaias:* LIII, 4 ff. Isaias here explains how Christ will be a victim offered in place of sinful man, "he hath borne our infirmities and carried our sorrows"; how he takes the place of the lamb of sacrifice; "he shall be led as a sheep to the slaughter, and shall be dumb as a lamb before his shearer."

a) And *this was explained by:*

(1) *Christ Himself* in the Gospel according to St. Matthew, XX, 28: "Even as the Son of Man has not come . . . but to give his life a redemption for many."

(2) *St. Paul to the Hebrews:* IX, 13: "For if the blood of goats and of oxen, and the ashes of an heifer being sprinkled, sanctify such as are defiled to the cleansing of the flesh, how much more shall the blood of Christ who by the Holy Ghost offered himself unspotted unto God, cleanse our conscience from dead works, to serve the living God?"

(3) *John the Baptist,* who looking at Christ, says: "Behold the Lamb of God who taketh away the sins of the world."

(a) *A Lamb,* the principal animal of sacrifice.

(b) *Who does what the animals* of sacrifice were supposed to do: Win God's friendship for mankind.

VI. The Great Sacrifice of the New Law was Calvary:

Note: This is the briefest possible explanation of the sacrifice of Calvary; fuller treatment with complete proofs is given in the treatise on the Mass.

A. **St. Paul** discusses at length in his Epistles the contrast between the incomplete sacrifices of the Hebrews and the age-long, perfect, and complete sacrifice of the New Law in which:

1. Christ, the Son of God, offers to His Father, the *perfect gift of His own life.*

2. *This life is destroyed* as a sign of God's complete dominion over life.

3. The Victim, Christ, *substitutes His life* for that of His human brothers and sisters, as the lives of the animals of sacrifice were imperfectly substituted for the Hebrews.

4. Since Christ is God, the value of the *sacrifice is infinite.*

5. Since Christ is also man, it is man's supreme gift to God. *Christ, the man, offers it for men.* "I lay down My life for My sheep."

6. He does this *voluntarily,* "I lay"; hence the Jews were merely the instruments of the sacrifice, though the cause of the death.

Note 1: Christ is eager to complete the sacrifice: "I have a Baptism wherewith I am to be baptized, and how am I straitened until it be accomplished." He returns voluntarily to Jerusalem knowing that He will be killed there. He allows soldiers in Gethsemane to capture Him after striking them to the earth to show His power over them.

Note 2: The Jews and Romans who killed Him, did so:
  a) Because they hated Him.
  b) And plotted to carry out His death, as He is an obstacle to their power and position.
  c) But though hating their motive, Christ permits their deed.
  d) And as He is slain by them, voluntarily offers His death as a Sacrifice to God for mankind.

Problems and Discussions

1. What significance has the ordinary human statement: I appreciate a gift most when it comes at the cost of a sacrifice?
2. Demonstrate to a non-Catholic that sacrifice is a natural instinct.
3. What argument could you draw from the fact that every important religion until Sixteenth-Century Protestantism contained the idea of sacrifice?
4. Do you think that a child who never heard the word *sacrifice* would show signs of that instinct:
  a) Toward parents?
  b) Toward God, when he learned about God?
5. Why does the word *sacrifice* usually suggest something brave and fine and difficult? e.g., sacrifice in a soldier, a mother, a hero or heroine.
6. List typical sacrifices found in ancient false religions.
7. Do you see any sacrificial significance in pagan incense? In pagan religious banquets?
8. A pagan, thinking the gods were angry with him, threw a beautiful ring into the sea. Why?
9. Before they drank, Romans and Greeks paused to pour a little of their wine on the ground in honor of the gods. Why?
10. If Christ is to be a priest "according to the order of Melchisedech," what does this imply? Was it true of Calvary? Draw the inevitable conclusion, if any.
11. Define a "scapegoat" and show that Christ was the fulfillment of the symbolic scapegoat of the Old Law.
12. Explain in detail why the greeting of St. John was accurate: "Behold the Lamb of God who taketh away the sins of the world."
13. Explain to a non-Catholic the sacrificial import of Calvary.
14. Can it be said that the cross was an altar?
15. Investigate from New and Old Testaments the passages referred to in the text.

Suggested Readings

Note: This reading list applies to Chapters VIII, IX, and X.

PAMPHLETS

The Queen's Work Press:
The Community Mass, Puetter, S.J.
Our High Mass, Hellriegel.
Catholic Truth Society:
The Saints of the Mass, Philipps.
What Is the Mass? Vaughan, S.J.
Explanation of the Prayers and Ceremonies of the Mass, Hallet.
At Mass, C. C. Martindale, S.J.
America Press:
The Unending Sacrifice, Reville.
The Liturgical Press:
My Sacrifice and Yours, Michel.
The Mass-Drama, Busch.
Paulist Press:
Modern Psychology and the Mass, O'Brien.
The Liturgy of the Mass, Messenger.

BOOKS

Grimaud, *My Mass* (Benziger).
Scott, *Holy Sacrifice of the Mass* (Kenedy).
D'Arcy, *The Mass and the Redemption* (Benziger Brothers).
Martindale, *Mind of the Missal* (Sheed and Ward).
Martindale, *Words of the Missal* (Sheed and Ward).
Boeser-Cannon, *The Mass Liturgy* (Bruce).
See the *Catholic Encyclopedia:* Mass; Sacrifice; *et passim.*

Chapter IX

MASS — II

I. **If** with Christ's sacrifice on Calvary, **the sacrifices of the New Law had been completed:**

    A. The Church and the religion that Christ established would have *no present sacrifice.*

    B. Men of the present would have *no gift or sacrifice* approved by God to give Him:

        1. For the sacrifices of the Old Law ended with Christ's Sacrifice on Calvary.

        2. The figures and types of the Old Law (sacrificial lamb, Paschal banquet) would have had no fulfillment in the religion of the New Law.

    C. Therefore the *religion of the New Law* would be:

        1. *Less satisfactory* to human instincts than the Old Law which preceded it.

        2. *Less perfect,* since lacking a permanent and present sacrifice.

II. **Christ** did not wish this; so He **gave men a permanent and present sacrifice:**

    A. That is the *same as that of Calvary.*

    B. Though in an *unbloody* form.

    C. Lasting *always.*

    D. *Accessible* to all.

Note: At this point, the Institution of Mass should be read: Matthew, XXVI, 26–28; Mark, XIV, 22–24; Luke, XXII, 19–20.

III. **The Last Supper is the First Mass** and the institution of that sacrifice which was to commemorate and continue Calvary.

    A. Christ takes *bread and wine,* the elements of Melchisedech's sacrifice. (He is becoming the "priest according to the order of Melchisedech.")

    B. What He is doing is *to be done always.* ("Thou art a priest *forever* according," etc.)

    C. *Through the instrumentality of others.* "Do this," is addressed to the Apostles. They are to continue what He has begun.

D. This is the *same body "which will be broken"* on Calvary; the *same blood "which will be shed"*; and this is done "for the remission of sins," one of the great purposes of sacrifice.

E. On Calvary, His *blood was separate from His body,* causing His death, so in the Last Supper:

　　a) He consecrates first the bread;

　　b) And then separately, He consecrates the wine;

　　c) To indicate a mystical separation of body and blood, representing (but not actually causing) His death.

F. Here, as on Calvary, *He is the priest,* who offers the sacrifice. Here as on Calvary, *He is the victim,* offered in Sacrifice.
　　　　　　"My body . . . My blood."

G. *Every word* He uses *has a sacrificial meaning* or connotation, suggests the sacrifices of the Old Law, looks forward to Calvary:

Body which is given . . . blood which is shed . . . blood of the New Testament (different from the blood of the Old, which was that of animals). . . . Which is shed for many (on Calvary) for the remission of sins (one of the purposes of sacrifice). . . . This is My body which is given *for you.*

H. He climaxes the sacrifice with *a sacrificial banquet,* as had been the case with the Paschal Lamb Sacrifice just completed. This was the **first Holy Communion.**

IV. **At the Last Supper,** Christ did briefly and essentially three things **that the Priest does in each Mass:**

A. *He offered bread and wine* to His Father.

B. *He consecrated them* with the words: This is My body . . . This is My blood.

C. *He gave Holy Communion* to those who had celebrated the banquet with Him.

V. Here we have the **three essential parts** of the Mass;

A. *Offertory.*

B. *Consecration.*

C. *Communion.*

VI. And **what Christ did at the Last Supper,** was also done **on Calvary:**

     A. Christ offered Himself to God, His Father.

     B. His body was separated from His blood.

     C. He gave Himself to be the life of the world.

VII. Hence Calvary, the Last Supper, and Mass are essentially the same, though numerically different.

     A. To the three essential acts of Offertory, Consecration, Communion, *the Church has added:*

        1. Beautiful and significant *prayers.*

        2. *Actions* suggesting or portraying the sacredness and solemnity of the sacrifice.

        3. *Readings from the Scriptures:* Psalms, epistles, gospels, prophecies.

VIII. **Historically:** What Christ did, and ordered to be done, **has been done ever since,** thus:

     A. Mass today is practically as it was *during the Crusades:* Prayers, vestments, order, canon.

     B. Mass during the Crusades was essentially and in most details the same as that said *by St. Augustine* (+ 430) and St. Gregory the Great (+ 604).

     C. Mass said by these saints was essentially the same as that said by the Christian priests as soon as they came *from the catacombs* (C. 300). Many of the prayers are identical.

     D. The *accidentals of the Mass* were in many cases taken straight from the Mass said in the catacombs:

        1. The altar contains *a relic* (part of the body of a martyr) because Mass in the catacombs was said on the tombs of the martyrs.

        2. The altar must be *stone,* or have a stone center, because those tombs were stone.

        3. The *candles* are used, among other reasons, because the catacombs were always dark.

Note: The Mass is represented in the catacombs by the faithful about a table on which are bread and wine and a fish. The fish was the Christian symbol for Christ, the Greek word, *Ichthus,* meaning fish; the letters standing thus: I, Jesus; Ch, Christ; Th, of God; U, the son; S, savior. Hence, the Mass of the catacombs had Christ, symbolized by the fish, as its center.

     E. The earliest Christian documents tell how *the first Christians did what Christ did* at the Last Supper:

1. Offered bread and wine.
2. Consecrated.
3. Gave Communion.
   Read in this connection, St. Paul to the Corinthians, I,
   XI, 23–29.

F. All the *main groups of heretics* until Luther's day retained
the Mass: Gnostics, Nestorians, Arians, Pelagians, Greeks;
only Protestantism gave it up, and many Episcopalians are
returning to it.

G. Therefore, Mass has been part of the Christian worship
from the beginning, and today is said not merely by all Catholic priests, but is part of the worship of all Christian bodies
except the Protestant.

IX. **The Importance of the Mass** may be indicated:
A. *By the hatred* of the Mass shown *by the enemies* of Christ
and His Church.

1. *Romans* accused the early Christians of sacrificing and eat-
ing a child at the Mass. This indicated that they understood
something of the significance but misunderstood the essence of
Mass. They tried by laws and persecutions to eliminate the
Christian "mysteries."

2. *Mohammedans* always attacked the Blessed Sacrament and
Mass.

3. *Early Protestantism* smashed the altars and broke the altar
stones.

4. The *atheists and deists* of the French Revolution made violent laws against priests and the Mass.

5. *Mexico and Russia* today practically outlaw the Mass.

B. *By the willingness of men to die* so that Mass could be said:

1. Romans found it easiest to capture the early Christians
when they were gathered for their "mysteries," Mass. This
did not deter the Christians.

2. The Irish during penal days said Mass in caves and behind
the hedges at peril of their lives.

3. England built hideaways in Catholic homes where Mass was
said when a price was put on priests' heads and confiscation
was visited on the householder.

4. Martyrs of the Mass were plentiful in the French Revolution, and are today in Mexico and Russia.

Problems and Discussions

1. Is there any indication in the architectural style of Protestant churches that Mass was intended to be said there?
2. Explain to a non-Catholic the full import and significance of the prophecy: "Thou art a priest forever according to the order of Melchisedech."
3. Could the prophecy of Malachy, "from the rising of the sun," etc., apply to anything else than the Mass? Does it apply to the Mass? Show this is geographically true.
4. If a non-Catholic said to you, "Mass began in the Eleventh Century," could you show him that he is wrong?
5. Early Protestantism called the Mass a "mummery." Why, if this were true, would it be true also of the Last Supper?
6. Trace in parallel columns all the essential factors that are identical in Calvary, the Last Supper, Mass.
7. Was the Church wise to add to the essential elements of the Mass (Offertory, Consecration, and Communion) the prayers, music, actions, readings, etc., of the Mass as it now is?
8. Could the Church, without destroying the Mass, eliminate these additions in case of necessity?
9. Show that the Mass contains all that is essential for a true sacrifice.
10. What arguments could you adduce from the fact that Mass was said for centuries before Protestantism.
11. Discuss this statement: The love of the believers and the hatred of the unbelievers proves the truth of the Mass.
12. What might have been in the mind of Christ as He instituted the Mass:
    a) Regarding His other prophecy: "I shall be with you all days, even to the consummation of the world"?
    b) Regarding the sacrileges which He foresaw?
    c) Regarding the satisfaction intelligent mankind would feel in the continuance of the sacrifice of Calvary to the end of time?
13. Why is the Mass of infinite value?
14. A man of Irish extraction is the descendant of ancestors who died or suffered intense persecution, confiscation of property and loss of citizenship, in order to attend Mass. He misses Mass regularly on Sunday. What is to be thought of him?
15. A young woman says: "I wish it had been my privilege to be present with the Holy Women on Calvary." What consolation could you offer her?

Chapter X

MASS — III

I. **The offering of the Sacrifice of the Mass makes the essential difference between Catholic and Protestant worship:**
   A. *Both agree* in the giving of *sermons.*
   B. Both agree *in sacred music.*
   C. They *separate* because the Catholic Church alone has *sacrifice.*

II. **Hence, a Catholic goes to Church:**
   A. *To offer with the priest a sacrifice,* humanly satisfying, divinely instituted and approved, perfect in Victim and High Priest, giving glory to God and grace to mankind.
   B. *To be present at the repetition of Calvary* and the Last Supper.
   C. *To reënact at Christ's command* what He did in those two places:
      1. In order *to offer supreme honor* to God.
      2. In order *to win tremendous graces* and blessings for self and for mankind.

Note: As much grace can actually be won for the soul and the world by the person assisting at Mass as if he had been:

   a) Present on Calvary.
   b) Present to receive Holy Communion from Christ at the Last Supper.

III. **Two general types** of Catholics assist at Mass:
   A. *The dull, ignorant, inert spectator,* who neither appreciates nor understands the sacrifice offered before him.

Note: He is like:

1. The ignorant element of the mob who watched the Crucifixion without hating Christ or approving of the crime; but equally lacking in understanding of what was offered and who offered.
2. The servants who prepared the supper chamber for the Last Supper and waited on the Apostles, without knowing what was occurring at that banquet.

   B. *The intelligent and appreciative Catholic,* who knows what the Mass means, why it is precious and important, and how to

offer it most effectively for himself and for others, and actually
offers the Mass together with the priest.

Note: He is like:

1. St. John, the Good Thief, the saintly women, the converted centurion
   on Calvary.
2. The devoted Apostles at the Last Supper.

IV. **The Mass** is not the sacrifice of the priest alone but **of priest and
people together:**

    A. The priest calls it *meum et vestrum sacrificium,* "my sacri-
fice and yours."

    B. He always *prays in the plural, Oremus, Orate, fratres,* etc.

    C. He may not, without special permission and special need,
say Mass *without a server* or alone.

    D. *The acolyte represents the congregation* and speaks in their
name. Originally the prayers of the priest were answered by
the people directly.

    E. In early times the *people* came up at the offertory to present
the priest with the bread and wine that he was later to
consecrate.

Note: The money collection at offertory time now takes the place of this
older and more complicated gift.

V. **Hence, people and priest united** offer to God this sacrifice of the
New Law. Christ is the great High Priest of every Mass. Priest
and people offer Mass with Him.

    A. **The priest offers the Mass:**

        1. *To honor and praise God:* who is King of the universe,
Father of us all, our Creator, and eventually our Judge.

        2. *To thank Him for His benefits:* of creation, preservation,
adoption, redemption, sanctification, and His special gifts to
the individuals and groups in the community.

        3. *To beg His forgiveness* for the sins of the human race: So
that the world may not be destroyed because of its sin, and
individuals may find pardon.

        4. *To win new graces* for the whole human race: both those
living on earth, and those in purgatory.

    B. *Usually the Mass is also offered:*

        1. In honor of *some special feast* of our Lord or our Lady or
of the saints.

2. *For some special intention* of the living and dead.

3. On Sundays and holydays, if said by the pastor, *for the welfare of the people.*

4. *To commemorate the ecclesiastical cycle* which runs from Advent with its expectation of Christ, through His life, passion, resurrection, and ascension to Pentecost and the coming of the Holy Spirit.

C. Hence *the importance of the congregation following the Mass* with the priest, and intelligently assisting him in the offering of the sacrifice:

1. *Uniting with the priest* in the actions of sacrifice.

2. *Praying with him* as he prays.

3. *Making the Mass* not merely a spectacle to be observed, enjoyed, or partially ignored, but *a sacrifice offered* for most important intentions.

4. *Making their own special intentions* for which the Mass is offered. Such intentions may be:

   a) *For themselves.*

   b) *For the living:* relatives, friends, dependents, associates, the Church, missions, the young, the tempted, the suffering, priests, etc.

   c) *For the dead:* relatives, friends, neglected souls, etc.

VI. To make this effective, **the following methods** may be employed:

A. *Before the Mass,* the individual should unite his intentions with those of the priest.

"My God, I offer You the Mass to honor and praise You, to acknowledge Your dominion over me and over the world, to thank You for Your favors especially . . . to beg pardon for my sins, especially . . . to obtain graces for myself, especially . . . to obtain graces for others, especially . . . to obtain release for the souls in Purgatory, especially. . . ."

B. *The use of the missal is invaluable.* This is the official prayer book of the Mass. Its value consists in the fact that:

1. It gives the individual *the same prayers* the priest says.

2. It brings out *the full meaning* of the Mass by making the individual come close to the actual words and actions of the priest.

3. Because the prayers and readings of the Mass are constantly changing, *it adds variety* to assistance at Mass.

4. It *prevents distractions.*

Note: At this point, those acquainted with the missal can be assigned to teach those not acquainted with the missal its use.

C. *United assistance adds value and beauty* to the Mass. "Where two or three are gathered together in My name, there am I in the midst of them."

1. *United prayer is more powerful* because it causes Christ to fulfill this promise.

2. *It adds* to the actual number of those offering *the prayers and actions of the Mass.*

3. This united assistance may be:

   a) Through the prayers of the Mass said together.

   b) Through the recitation of the responses of the acolyte and the union with the prayers of the priest where this is permitted.

   c) Through the singing of appropriate hymns.

   d) Through the recitation of appropriate prayers.

VII. **Intelligent assistance** at Mass includes the following elements:

Note: This may be worked out as problems by the students. The prayers the priest says as he uses the vestments indicate their purpose. These are in every missal. Through a brief review, the instructor may carry the students to see the significance:

a) In vestments.

b) In the construction of the altar.

c) In the ceremonies and actions of the priest.

A. Briefly: **The vestments** are ancient in form, suggesting the garments worn by Christ at the Last Supper and at the Passion. Symbolic meanings have been attached to them:

1. *The amice* is the helmet worn by the priest going forth to do battle for the people.

2. *The alb* is the white robe:

   a) Suggesting the robe put upon Christ by Herod.

   b) The white Roman toga used by the earliest priests.

   c) The seamless robe of Christ.

   d) The shining purity that should characterize a priest.

3. *The cincture* signifies the ropes that bound the Savior.

4. *The stole,* besides suggesting the ropes of the Passion, is

the distinctive garment of the priest, worn in all his priestly functions: confession, the sacraments, preaching.

5. *The maniple,* another cord binding Christ.

6. *The chasuble,* marked with a cross, symbolic of the cross carried by the first High Priest of the New Law.

  a) Changes color to denote the type of feast:

    (1) White: Christ, the Father, our Lady, confessors, and virgins.

    (2) Red: The Holy Ghost, martyrs.

    (3) Black: Good Friday and for the dead.

    (4) Purple: Seasons of mourning, and penance.

    (5) Green: The Sundays after Pentecost and following Epiphany.

Note: The priest dressed in his vestments is set aside even by his garments from all ordinary pursuits, and marked as belonging to God's official work.

B. **The Altar:** is also ancient in form and design:

  1. A central *stone* of sacrifice.

  2. Contains the *relic* of a martyr.

  3. *Candles* must burn:

    a) To recall the darkness of the catacombs.

    b) As a symbol of faith, burning like a flame.

    c) To light a welcome to the coming Christ.

  4. *Linen cloths* cover the altar:

    a) Recalling the cloth on the table of the Last Supper.

    b) The winding sheet with which Christ's body was wrapped following the Passion.

  5. *Special altar furniture* includes:

    a) The *missal* on its stand.

    b) The *cruets* for wine and water.

    c) The *towel and basin* for the washing of hands.

    d) The *bell* to indicate the chief parts of the Mass.

  6. *The crucifix* over the altar, to recall Calvary.

  7. *The tabernacle* (not necessary for an altar or Mass) in which Christ remains after the sacrifice.

C. *Every action or gesture* of the Mass is deeply significant. There is no meaningless or purposeless word or act. These can well be studied in detail, as an assignment or special discussion.

Problems and Discussions

1. If a Catholic told you that Mass bored him, what could you deduce from this remark? What suggestions could you offer him?
2. Could you suggest a better expression for attendance at Mass than, "hearing Mass"?
3. Explain to a non-Catholic something of the meaning of the phrase, *meum et vestrum sacrificium.*
4. What are the four great purposes of the Mass?
5. Is Mass ever offered to a saint? Analyze the prayer (oration) of a saint's feast to show that your answer is correct.
6. Give your opinion of the following ways of assisting at Mass:
    a) The recitation of the rosary.
    b) Reading from Thomas à Kempis.
    c) Saying the Thirty Day Prayer.
    d) Reciting the Penitential Psalms.
    e) Meditating on Calvary.
    f) Imagining oneself at the Last Supper with Christ about to consecrate and give Holy Communion.
    g) Following the actions of the priest and uniting oneself with them.
7. Discuss the correctness of the following common statement: "I can worship God just as well in a forest under the trees as I can in a church at Mass."
8. A non-Catholic tells you that the priest's vestments are silly and showy. What would you answer him?
9. In view of the principle of offering Mass together with the priest, how could the term "co-priest" as applied to laypeople be explained?
10. What would constitute a satisfactory preparation for Mass?
11. Describe possible mental processes of an intelligent Catholic at Mass.
12. Describe possible mental processes of an unintelligent Catholic at Mass?
13. Take an altar apart for a non-Catholic and make clear its use.
14. Why is Latin instead of the vernacular used at Mass?
15. Could you explain to a non-Catholic the expression: "It is the Mass that matters"?

Chapter XI

THE CHURCH AND HISTORY

I. **Today the Catholic Church is,** to the superficial observer,
    A. *One of a series of Churches:*
      1. All claiming to teach with Christ's commission.
      2. Or at least claiming to show men the way to higher life.
    B. *One of a series of organizations;* e.g., nations, associations, groups, societies, all offering service to the human race.

II. This fact confuses the superficial observer:
    A. There are so many churches all claiming to be true, yet all teaching different things; so many groups offering aid and comfort to mankind, that he gets the idea that all religions must be about the same and all equally important or unimportant.

III. **Yet today the Catholic Church:**
    A. *Exists more strongly* than ever.
    B. Is *spread* throughout the world.
    C. Exercises the *most profound influence* both upon Catholics and those outside the Church.
    D. *Continues its work of teaching,* charity, guidance.
    E. *Despite terrific attacks* made upon it:
      1. Through *Roman emperors.*
      2. *Powerful heretics,* like Arius, Nestorius, Pelagius.
      3. *Great anti-Catholic movements* like Mohammedanism, the Barbarian Invasions, the Tartar Conquests.
      4. The schism and departure of the *Greek church.*
      5. The fierce attack of the *Protestant Revolution* that took away England, Scotland, Wales, Northern Germany, Scandinavia, part of France and Bohemia, part of Holland.
      6. The relentless and bitter attacks of *pagans and atheists and skeptical scientists and philosophers* during the past 150 years. From Voltaire to Darrow, through the brilliant and the merely smart, this attack has gone forward: Kant, Schopenhauer, Nietzsche; the Encyclopedists, the Modernists, the Higher Critics; Haeckel, Spencer, Huxley, and their multiplied successors.

IV. Hence **the Catholic Church**:
    A. *Continues its career,* numerous, powerful, effective;
    B. *Despite terrific assaults* and varied attacks and the fact that
    millions of its followers have left it and millions of others have
    done all in their power to stop its work.

V. **The intelligent Catholic, then, realizes**:
    A. That he is a *member of a Church* which is *so venerable* in years
    that most modern European nations are its children.
    B. That compared to it, *all other Christian denominations* are par-
    venus.
    C. That *his Church has been persecuted,* attacked, and discredited
    for almost 1900 years and is still stronger than ever.
        1. Its Founder was regarded as a failure and crucified.
        2. The Athenians laughed at St. Paul when he preached the
        resurrection.
        3. The powerful Roman Empire and the powerful Jewish people
        persecuted the Church violently.
        4. Wave after wave of heretics swept over it, and were lost in
        history: Gnostics, Arians, Pelagians, Nestorians, Lollards, Ana-
        baptists, Albigenses, Hussites, all once powerful, promising to
        subdue the Church, and rapidly disappearing.
        5. Luther and the Reformers declared the Church dead and
        called up armies to fight it.
        6. Voltaire promised to destroy "the infamous thing."
        7. Modern countries: France, Germany, England, Spain, Por-
        tugal, Russia, the Central Americas, Mexico, have made war
        upon it.
        8. Modern unbelieving science and philosophy have treated it as
        obsolete and dead.
    D. That *Christ promised His Church that it would never fail* and
    never be overcome by its enemies:
    "The gates of Hell shall not prevail against it. . . . I shall be
    with you all days, even to the end of the world."
    E. That *Christ said the Church was to speak with His voice* and
    possess His authority:
    "He that heareth you heareth Me; and he that despiseth you,
    despiseth Me."
    F. That outside the Catholic Church, *the world is split and torn
    into the most opposing organizations:*
        1. *Into religions that agree in nothing:* Episcopalians and Mor-

mons; Quakers and Unitarians; Holy Rollers, Presbyterians, Salvation Army, Seventh Day Adventists, Lutherans, Christian Scientists, and hundreds of others.

2. *Into schools of thought that are absolutely contradictory.*

Note: This will be seen at length in the History of Philosophy courses, and in the study of developing scientific theories and hypotheses.

    G. That *the Catholic Church* is in *de facto* possession of:

      1. *Historic age,* and the rights of seniority.

      2. *Immediate connection with Christ* and the Apostles on whom He established His Church.

      3. An existence that in the past has *withstood* the fiercest attack without yielding or failure.

      4. *A tremendous body of followers* today larger than any religious group in the world and bigger than all the Protestant bodies combined.

VI. When the Catholic Church was founded, 1900 years ago, these nations were the important nations of the then civilized world:

    A. Rome; Persia; Greece, as a Roman province; Judea, also a Roman province.

    B. Today all are gone, and the Church remains. Rome has gone through change after change; modern Persia bears no connection with the Persia of that day. Greece has been changed a score of times. Judea is a race without a land or a nation.

VII. **To replace these nations,** the following came into existence:

    A. **France:** For centuries it was called "the eldest daughter of the Church." The barbarian tribes welded together by Clovis (+ 511), formed into a nation under Louis XI (+ 1483) but had been Christianized by the Catholic Church under St. Remegius (+ 533).

    B. **England:** The Early Britons, contemporaries of Rome, were driven out by the Anglo-Saxons who amalgamated with the Normans (1066–1400). But England was Christianized by the Catholic Church under St. Augustine (+ 604).

    C. **Germany:** Barbaric tribes were Christianized by St. Boniface (+ 755) and formed the Empire under Charlemagne (+ 814).

    D. **Russia:** Once more barbaric tribes were Christianized by the Catholic Church under SS. Cyril and Methodius (+ 869).

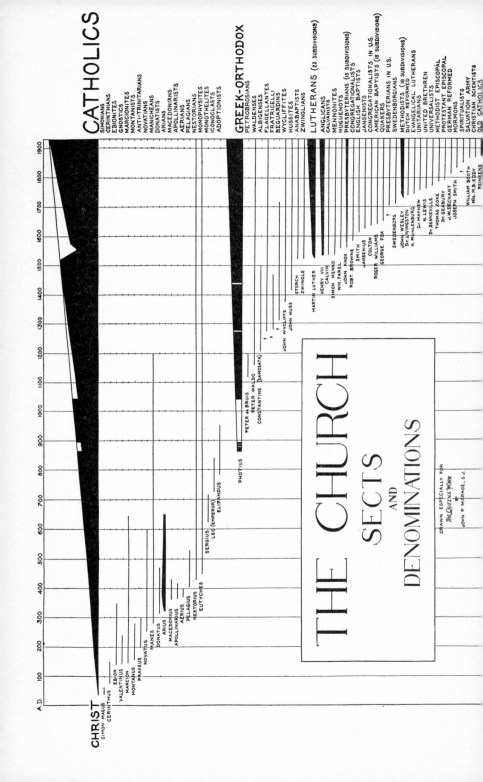

THE CHURCH
SECTS
AND
DENOMINATIONS

DRAWN ESPECIALLY FOR
The Queen's Work
BY
JOHN P. MARKOE, S.J.

CATHOLICS

CHRIST
SIMON MAGUS
CERINTHUS
EBION
VALENTINUS
MARCION
MONTANUS
PRAXEUS
NOVATUS
MANES
DONATUS
ARIUS
MACEDONIUS
APOLLINARIUS
AERIUS
PELAGIUS
NESTORIUS
EUTYCHES
SERGIUS
LEO (EMPEROR)
ELIPANDUS

SIMONIANS
CERINTHIANS
EBIONITES
GNOSTICS
MARCIONITES
MONTANISTS
ANTI-TRINITARIANS
NOVATIANS
MANICHEANS
DONATISTS
ARIANS
MACEDONIANS
APOLLINARISTS
AERIANS
PELAGIANS
NESTORIANS
MONOPHYSITES
MONOTHELITES
ICONOCLASTS
ADOPTIONISTS

GREEK-ORTHODOX
PHOTIUS
PETER de BRUS
PETER WALDO
CONSTANTINE (SAMOSATA)
JOHN WYCLIFFE
JOHN HUSS
STORCH
ZWINGLE

PETROBROSIANS
WALDENSES
ALBIGENSES
FLAGELLANTES
FRATRICELLI
BEGUARDINS
WYCLIFFITES
HUSSITES
ANABAPTISTS
ZWINGLIANS

LUTHERANS (22 subdivisions)
MARTIN LUTHER
HENRY VIII
CALVIN
SIMON MENNO
WM. FAREL
JOHN KNOX
ROBT. BROWNE
SMITH
JANSENIUS
COLTON
ROGER WILLIAMS
GEORGE FOX
SWEDENBORG
JOHN WESLEY
Dr. LIVINGSTON
H. MUHLENBURG
Dr. MAYHEW
N. LEWIS
Dr. BENNEVILLE
THOMAS COKE
Dr. SEABURY
J.W. DECHANT
JOSEPH SMITH
WILLIAM BOOTH
Mrs. M.B. EDDY
RENKENS

ANGLICANS
CALVINISTS
MENNONITES
HUGUENOTS
PRESBYTERIANS (15 SUBDIVISIONS)
CONGREGATIONALISTS
ENGLISH BAPTISTS
JANSENIST
CONGREGATIONALISTS IN U.S.
AMERICAN BAPTISTS (18 SUBDIVISIONS)
QUAKERS
PRESBYTERIANS IN U.S.
SWEDENBORGIANS
METHODISTS (16 SUBDIVISIONS)
DUTCH REFORMED
EVANGELICAL LUTHERANS
UNITARIANS
UNITED BRETHREN
UNIVERSALISTS
METHODIST EPISCOPAL
PROTESTANT EPISCOPAL
GERMAN REFORMED
MORMONS
SPIRITUALISTS
SALVATION ARMY
CHRISTIAN SCIENTISTS
OLD CATHOLICS

A.D. | 100 | 200 | 300 | 400 | 500 | 600 | 700 | 800 | 900 | 1000 | 1100 | 1200 | 1300 | 1400 | 1500 | 1600 | 1700 | 1800 | 1900

This chart indicates at a glance that the Catholic Church has always been and is the one and only true Church of Christ on earth.

The chart represents in a graphical manner the important historical facts pertaining to the various churches that have claimed and in some cases still do claim to be the true Church of Christ.

The vertical lines mark the centuries of the Christian Era. The horizontal lines represent the more important of the hundreds of religious denominations that have come into existence during the past nineteen hundred years. These lines began at the dates when the respective sects arose and continue throughout the years of their existence. When a denomination has died out the line representing it ends. The average approximate increase in strength of the sects is shown by the changing width of their respective lines. A line one-half inch wide represents 60,000,000 members. This scale holds for all denominations having at least 1,000,000 members. Those having less than this number are shown as having 1,000,000 members, because lines representing their true strength would scarcely be visible. At the left of these lines appear the names of the founders of the various denominations.

Beneath the Catholic Church, and separating it from the sects, are shown the ecumenical or general councils whose judgments have condemned the doctrines of these as not having been taught by Christ and consequently false.

History states that Christ founded only one Church that was to continue in the world until the end of time, and against which the gates of hell would never prevail. Therefore that Church founded by Christ must be in the world today, and history points it out as the Catholic Church. The Catholic Church is the only Church in existence today that can trace its organization back to Christ and the Apostles. Therefore it must be His Church.

E. **The United States:** Founded as a nation, 1776; had seen as its first explorers, Catholics like Columbus and his successors; as its first missionaries: Franciscans with Columbus; Jesuits in Northern New York and Mississippi Valley; Franciscans in California and New Mexico and the Southwest; among its pioneers the Catholics of Maryland.

F. The countries which ceased to exist did not destroy the Catholic Church with their fall. The new countries formed out of the invasions of the Barbarians were converted by the Church and under its guidance made modern Europe.

VIII. Any man considering the question is faced with **these historical alternatives:**

A. *Either the Catholic Church is historically* the Church of Christ.

B. *Or there is no Church of Christ;* it disappeared and Christ's guarantee failed.

IX. **Christ guaranteed His Church would last:**

A. "Thou art Peter and upon this Rock I shall build My Church, and the gates of hell shall not prevail against it."

    1. This means:

      a) The Church has the unshaken firmness of a rock.

      b) Certainly no power on earth can overcome it, since hell will not be able to do so.

B. "Behold I am with you all days, even to the consummation of the world."

    1. Christ will stay with His Church.

    2. Forever, till the world ends.

C. "Who heareth you heareth Me."

D. Hence, if the Church which the world heard was teaching things not true, Christ's voice would be deceiving His followers.

X. **But for 1500 years** from the death of Christ:

A. The Catholic Church has had *an uninterrupted existence.*

B. *Other Churches rose and disappeared* during the course of this existence.

C. *Often, practically, it alone existed.*

D. *After 1500 years, the Protestant churches* were established claiming:

    1. That the Catholic Church was absolutely wrong.

2. That they were beginning again to teach the truth of Christ, not taught for 1200 years.

E. *After 1800 years, Methodism,* Mormonism, Christian Science arose.

F. Therefore:

1. Either the Catholic Church was the true Church established by Christ and given His promises and guarantee.

2. Or the promises and guarantees of Christ failed, and no Church is His true Church.

   a) All Churches except the Catholic Church failed; i.e., the gates of hell prevailed against the others.

   b) Or they arose too late to have Christ give His guarantee to them.

Note: All founders of other Christian Churches:

a) *Either were Catholics themselves:* e.g., Arius, Nestorius, Pelagius, Photius, Luther, Henry VIII, John Knox, Calvin (all but two were priests).

b) *Left the Catholic Church* to found a new church centuries after Christ finished His work.

c) *Or had ancestors* who were Catholic.

XI. **Therefore, compared to the Catholic Church:**

A. *All European nations are young,* most of them her children. Catholic bishops and prelates were chancellors and prime ministers of most of the young nations.

B. *All Europe was Christianized by the Catholic Church,* i.e., brought by it from barbarism to civilization. Protestantism found a Europe already civilized and converted.

C. *All non-Catholic religious founders:*

1. *Lived centuries after Christ* gave His Apostles His promise and guarantee.

2. *Broke away* from the Catholic Church.

3. *Showed no proofs* that God wanted a new religion, and that the Catholic Church had so far failed that the "gates of Hell had prevailed against it."

4. *Assumed but did not prove* their divine commission to change a faith and Church that dated back to Christ.

XII. **Modern unbelief,** whether scientific, religious, philosophical, moral, economic (Materialistic evolution, Christian Science, Kantianism, Birth Controllers, Communists):

A. *Have no historic connection with Christ,* nor His guarantee.
B. Have in their brief careers *changed their positions* and teachings again and again.
C. Will fade away as the other enemies of the Church faded.

Problems and Discussions

1. Why was Cardinal Gibbons right when he called the Catholic Church, even for non-Catholics, "the Faith of Our Fathers"?
2. Historically for 1900 years, the Catholic Church has never had to change one of its doctrines. Does this bear out Christ's guarantee? Explain.
3. Why can we call most Protestant religions, parvenu religions?
4. Discuss the statement: "The Church is the mother of modern Europe."
5. Discuss the common statement: "Religion like everything else has to improve with time."
6. Give a rapid historical survey of the rise of European nations and show their age compared with that of the Catholic Church.
7. Is there any vital connection between Christ's statement: "I will be with you all days," and the unfailing youth of the Church?
8. Date definitely the beginnings of most modern Protestant groups. Where, if they were really Christ's Church, was the Church of Christ before they were founded?
9. Could you argue from history (which repeats itself) that most modern religions and forms of unbelief will eventually disappear as the religions of the past did?
10. If the Catholic Church is "actually in possession of the field," is there anything mistaken about some Catholic laymen's attitude of being constantly afraid to defend their religion?
11. List some of the chief enemies and some of the most violent attacks upon the Catholic Church. Would it humanly seem that any of them was likely to succeed in crushing the Church?
12. Is it true that the religions outside the Catholic Church contradict one another?
13. Show that anti-Christian scientific theories contradict one another.
14. A Jew argues: "If your argument is true, then all the world should be Jewish, for the Catholic Church broke away from the Jewish religion." Would his argument be valid if: The Jews expected a redeemer who was going to change their religion and government? If the Jewish religion was an "incomplete" religion expecting its completion in its Messias? If the Jews rejected the Messias when He came, fulfilling the prophecies, completing the types and prototypes, and offering them His leadership and His religion with its guarantee?

15. A Christian Scientist argues: "But Christian Science does wonderful cures. Therefore it must be correct."

Suggested Readings

PAMPHLETS

Paulist Press:
Outline of Church History, Shahan.
Testimony of History for the Roman Catholic Church.
The Story of the Church, Keppel.

BOOKS

Kurth, *The Church at the Turning Points of History* (Naegele).
Parsons, *Some Lies and Errors of History* (Ave Maria Press).
Desmond, *Mooted Questions of History* (Benziger).
Zahm, *What the Church Has Done for Science* (Notre Dame Press).
Devas, *Key to the World's Progress* (Longmans).
Belloc, *Catholic Church and History* (Calvert Series) (Macmillan).
Laux, *Church History* (Benziger).
Rowe, *Historical Struggles for the Faith* (Herder).

Chapter XII

THE CHURCH AND THE PRESENT

I. No man lives in the past. Hence Catholics, proud of the age and
traditions of their church, must be keenly alive to **the Church as
it exists today.** The Church's place in the world today is of fundamental importance, not alone in its mission to souls but in what
it does for all mankind.

II. **The guarantee of Christ that His Church would never die is
vividly fulfilled today.** Despite its numberless enemies, it is
more alive and flourishing than ever.

Note: All the Church's modern enemies have predicted its immediate death:

> 1. *Voltaire* and his followers, the writers of the Encyclopedia,
> campaigned 150 years ago to "destroy the infamous thing."
> When the French Revolution broke out, they were sure they
> had succeeded.
> 2. *The Materialistic Group* (mid-nineteenth century), Huxley,
> Spencer, Haeckel, and others, were convinced its collapse was
> to come within 50 years.
> 3. *The Modernist Group* (Renan, Strauss, Tyrrell, Loisy) de-
> clared that the Church would either have to change or die.
> Some of them joined the "Old Catholic Church," now already
> largely extinct. Others simply disappeared into oblivion, while
> the Church goes on.
> 4. *The Socialist Group* felt that the Church would end its work
> by the close of the nineteenth century. (In Bellamy's *Looking
> Backwards,* Socialism is established and Catholicity dead by
> 1900.)

III. Today the Church shows **its unfailing youth and power:**

> A. *The Messages of the Popes* are the most important news in
> the world's newspapers.
> > 1. Front pages are given them in every civilized country (ex-
> > cept Russia, where they are not allowed to appear).

2. They treat the world's most important questions and get instant consideration by all the experts, whether they concern marriage, politics, economics, or any other subject.
3. The Pope, with only a trifle of temporal power, is admitted even by non-Catholics to be the most important religious moral and social leader in the world.
4. Public opinion and world politics forced the return to him of his temporal independence. He is above and beyond any idea of mere nationality and belongs to the world.

B. Today as always, *converts continue to come into the Church* in astonishing numbers.
1. Great groups like the Episcopalian ministers who have come in since the days of the Oxford Movement.
2. Notable individuals in every line of life: Sigrid Undset, Noble prize winner; Bishop Kinsman, of the Episcopalian Church; John Moody, financier; Admiral Benson, of the U. S. Navy; and hundreds of thinkers and literary men and women.

C. While *missionary activity is greater* than ever before:
1. Every pagan country, even the most desolate and isolated, is covered by groups of Catholic missionaries.
2. Thousands of Catholic converts are made each year.
3. Whole nations, like those of the Uganda in Africa, are today made Catholic.
4. New missions are constantly being established.
5. New Missionary Orders are being added to the already existing ones to carry on the conversions of the world: Franciscan Missionaries of Mary, Maryknoll Fathers and Sisters, Techny Fathers and Sisters, Columban Fathers, Holy Cross Sisters, etc.

IV. Hence, **the Church today is a world power,** international in character, yet made up of loyal citizens of every nation.
A. *The Church is the true League of Nations:*
1. Its hierarchy of *bishops is made up of every nationality* and every racial group: American, European, Oriental, African. Recently the Pope insisted upon a native clergy and a native hierarchy even in newly converted countries.
B. Its *members exist in every land.*
1. Compare this fact with the purely national character of

Anglicanism, Lutheranism, Christian Science, Swedenbor-
gianism, Mormonism, and the geographically circumscribed
character of the Protestant bodies. The Oriental religions are
almost all purely national in composition.

C. A traveler *in any part of the world finds in the Catholic
Church,* with its priests, worship, Mass, sacraments, identical
truths and practices.

D. The moral and spiritual *influence of the Church makes it
world wide* as not even the Roman Empire or the British Empire was world wide.

    1. Yet this is achieved and held:

      a) Without force of any kind. Contrast the missionary con-
quests of the Church with the territorial conquests of the
nations through force of arms. Note how when rebellions
and revolutions took, for example, South America from
Spain and Portugal, it did not take Catholics from the
Church.

      b) Among people the most diversified in racial character-
istics and backgrounds: Irish and French; Americans of
North and South America; Chinese and American Indians;
Hindus and natives of Uganda, etc. The most powerful
empires did not succeed in welding together the independent nations into a homogeneous group; the Catholic
Church holds these diversified people united in faith and
worship.

      c) With a *faith that admits no compromises* and conces-
sions in any essentials, no matter what the national differences. Today even national liturgies, that is, worship in
the national tongue, is not permitted to newly converted
races.

      d) With a *moral law difficult and exacting* and often op-
posed to age-old national practice; e.g., strict marriage
laws for groups that had practised polygamy and divorce.
Laws of abstinence to peoples accustomed to self-indul-
gence. Forgiveness and charity to warlike people.

      e) With *no power of coercion* and no visible punishment to
be a sanction for its laws and orders. Only supernatural
and invisible penalties follow the Catholic who rebels; e.g.,
excommunication, loss of the sacraments, the threat of
eternal ruin.

V. Today the Catholic Church is still the dominant religious body, even
in America as the official statistics show:

MEMBERSHIP OF
LEADING DENOMINATIONS IN THE UNITED STATES
1 9 2 6

CENSUS OF RELIGIOUS BODIES
DEPARTMENT OF COMMERCE

Denomination	Total Number of Members	Per Cent of Total
All denominations	54,576,346	100.0
1. Roman Catholic*	18,605,003	34.1
2. Jewish**	4,081,242	7.5
3. Methodist Episcopal***	4,080,777	7.5
4. Southern Baptist	3,524,378	6.5
5. Negro Baptists	3,196,623	5.9
6. M. E. South	2,487,694	4.6
7. Presbyterian, U. S. A.	1,894,030	3.5
8. Protestant Episcopal	1,859,086	3.4
9. Disciples of Christ	1,377,595	2.5
10. Northern Baptist	1,289,966	2.4
11. United Lutheran	1,214,340	2.2
12. Lutheran Mo. Synod	1,040,275	1.9
13. Congregational	881,696	1.6
14. African M. E.	545,814	1.0
15. Latter-Day Saints	542,194	1.0
16. Norw. Lutheran	496,707	0.9
17. A. M. E. Zion	456,813	0.8
18. Presb. U. S.	451,043	0.8
19. Churches of Christ	433,714	0.8
All other	6,117,356	11.2

*The figures on the chart, though higher than the Government figures, seem to give
a more accurate picture of the growth of the Catholic Church. They are based, for the
years 1790–1920, on the scholarly work of Gerald Shaughnessy *Has the Immigrant Kept
the Faith?* the most reliable book published on this subject.

**The Jewish Congregations do not appear on the chart because prior to 1926 the
census of their members was admittedly incomplete.

***On the chart the non-Catholic bodies are treated as "families" — that is, the
19 denominations of Methodists are united to form one "family" of Methodists; the
18 denominations of Baptists form one "family"; the 12 denominations of Lutherans
form one "family"; etc.

The figures for these bodies were taken from the reports of the Bureau of Census
of Religious Bodies, Department of Commerce, of 1890, 1906, 1916, and 1926. The
figures are estimated backwards prior to 1890.

Religions of the World run thus:
Catholics: 351,500,000
Confucianists: 315,600,000
Hindus: 230,150,000
Mohammedans: 209,000,000
Protestants (all sects): 205,900,000
Buddhists: 150,180,000
Greek Orthodox: 144,000,000
Animists (African primitive religions): 135,650,000
Taoists: 35,000,000
Shintoists: 25,000,000
Jews: 15,650,000
Miscellaneous: 50,570,000

VI. The Catholic Church continues its work:

A. *Able to create sufficient enthusiasm* among its members for the work it is doing to cause:

1. *Thousands of young men* to take up that work as priests and religious:

   a) Without families of their own.

   b) Or the hope of temporal wealth or success.

2. *Thousands of young women* to take up this work:

   a) Bind themselves by vows of poverty, chastity, and obedience.

   b) Consecrate their lives to charity, education, care for the poor, sick, needy, etc.

   c) Without salary or family or the world's important pleasures or rewards.

B. *With vast energy and activity.*

1. Not merely *the mother of hospitals,* founded first under Catholic inspiration; but today:

   a) With by far the *largest group of private hospitals in America;* handling every type of need and illness.

   b) With a constantly growing group of *magnificent hospitals in every civilized country* in the world.

Note: When the French Masons drove out the teaching sisters, they allowed the nursing sisters to remain at their hospital posts. This policy has been observed elsewhere; religious exiles did not always include nursing nuns and brothers.

   c) With a constantly increasing *service of the sick in the missions.*

2. And it operates and controls *every type of refuge* for every type of sufferer:

a) *The orphan.* In civilized and pagan lands, the orphanage is one of the first concerns of the Church.

b) *The fallen woman.* Institutions like the Houses of the Good Shepherd restore the unfortunate woman to her standing in the community and her hope of a future. This is a unique Catholic work, like the work of the Savior for the Magdalen and the woman taken in adultery.

c) *For the old poor.* The houses of the Little Sisters of the Poor and similar institutions are world-famous.

d) *For the blind, deaf, insane, poor,* etc.

C. *Intellectually powerful.* In spite of the fact that the Church is and will always be:

1. Largely the Church of the poor.
2. Continuously persecuted.
3. With its educational enterprises frequently stopped, its schools confiscated, and its teaching orders abolished.

Note: This was done during the Reformation days when many of its universities, e.g., Cambridge, Oxford, Heidelberg, etc., were taken away; in Mexico at least three different times; in Spain within the past few years; in France at the beginning of the present century; in Italy and Portugal to some extent; for three centuries in England, Ireland, and Scotland, and parts of Holland.

4. With no state taxes in America and in most European countries for its schools, though Catholics help through their taxes to support state schools.

a) *Its seminaries* train yearly thousands of young priests who compose the best educated body of men in the world.

b) In America *its educational system alone included* (in 1930):

    21 Universities,
  141 Colleges,
  400 Schools of Nursing,
2,128 High Schools,
7,923 Elementary Schools.

VII. Today as always **the Catholic Church** in the face of a changing world with all the persecutions, opposition, doubts and denials, **still continues its work:**

A. *Announcing the message of Christ* to the world.

B. *Offering the sacrifice of the Mass.*

C. *Serving men* through the sacraments.

D. *Leading them the sure way to heaven* and a certain eternity.

E. *Struggling against sin* and evil.

F. *Working for virtue* and truth.

G. And constantly concerned with the *promotion of the Kingdom of Christ* on earth.

H. And it does this with an *effectiveness* that:

    1. *Inspires the admiration* of the impartial observer.

    2. *And wins the consistent hatred* of the men who would have hated Christ.

Problems and Discussions

1. If after all the prophecies of collapse and the persecutions against it the Church still exists and flourishes, what argument could be drawn about the prophecies of its present enemies?

2. On what important subjects has the Pope recently spoken?

3. Does any individual compare in spiritual influence and authority with the Pope? Does he seem to possess this influence because of his own personal qualifications or because of his position as head of the Catholic Church?

4. Discuss the statement: People are always blaming the Church because it is easier to live outside it; yet converts join the Church in spite of the fact that it is hard to live inside it.

5. Could the Catholic Church because of its charities claim the title of the Greatest Mother in the World?

6. On a map indicate the character of the world-wide spread of the Church.

7. How does the missionary activity of the Church inevitably flow from Christ's command: "Go, teach all nations"?

8. Describe the international character of a Eucharist Congress.

9. Is this a true statement: Traveling around the world, a Catholic scarcely ever need to miss Mass on Sunday.

10. Indicate from your own city the extent and variety of Catholic charity and humanitarian activities.

11. What argument could one draw from the Church's charity, based on Christ's test: "By their fruits you shall know them"?

12. Has any other organization so united in ideas and practice as diversified a group of nations and races as that which makes up the Catholic Church?

13. A historian argues: "The Catholic Church kept medieval Europe

Catholic because of the union of Church and State and the power of the sword." If this is true, show that Church of today and the past 150 years should have fallen to pieces.

14. List the religious orders of men and women working in your city.
15. Discuss this statement: "No form of human need or misery falls outside the service of the modern Catholic Church."
16. Why do persecutors of the Church always attack and try to destroy its educational enterprises?
17. Is the spiritual work of the Church essentially changed or modified from what it was during the Middle Ages?

Suggested Readings

PAMPHLETS

The Queen's Work Press:
Whose Country Is This? Lord, S.J.
The Paulist Press:
Why Ronald Knox Became a Catholic, Conway, C.S.P.
Catholic Truth Society:
The Martyrs of Uganda, Streicher.
Miguel Pro, Rimmer, S.J.
Catholicism and the Future, Benson.

BOOKS

Windle, *The Church and Science* (Herder).
Guilday, *The Catholic Church in Contemporary Europe* (Kenedy).
Johnson, *One Lord, One Faith* (Sheed and Ward).
Dawson, *The Modern Dilemma* (Sheed and Ward).
Belloc, *Survivals and New Arrivals* (Macmillan).
Noyes, *The Torchbearers* (Epic poem) (Stokes).

Chapter XIII

THE CHURCH AS CHRIST'S REPRESENTATIVE — I

I. **The Catholic has an attitude** toward his Church entirely different from the attitude taken by any other religious group in the world. He thinks of it:

    A. **Not merely as an organization.**

      1. The Church, regarded *just as an institution, is supreme* among all the world organizations.

        a) With the advantages of democratic and monarchical governments combined:

          (1) It is a *democracy* in which any man may aspire to be bishop, cardinal, or pope.

Note: Most American bishops are taken from the families of moderate means, often from poor families. Popes have arisen from relatively poor families; e.g., Pius X, and the present Pius XI.

          (2) *With councils* meeting at intervals (general, national, and provincial) and *representing the whole body of the faithful.*

          (3) *Yet monarchical in government;* with the Pope as the supreme ruler (though elected) and bishops as princes (yet chosen from the lower clergy on the basis of merit), and with authority received from God.

"All power is given to Me in heaven and on earth; go, therefore, and teach the gospel to every creature."

"Who heareth you, heareth Me."

"I will give you the keys of the Kingdom of Heaven."

        b) With an *international* (Catholic in the broad sense of the word) *outlook;* yet carefully divided into groups of nations, provinces, cities, parishes.

          (1) The Church universal, with the pope and his counselors at its center.

          (2) The national hierarchies, with primates.

          (3) The provinces, with archbishops.

          (4) The dioceses, with bishops and their canons.

(5) Deaneries, with their deans.

(6) Parishes, with their pastors, directly serving the people.

c) *A common language,* uniting all the churches.

Note the futile struggle outside the Church to develop an international language similar to what the Church possesses in Latin.

d) *With religious orders* established for the individual needs of humanity, all working under superiors in close coöperation with Rome:

(1) For teaching.

(2) For missionary work.

(3) For charity.

(4) For hospitals.

(5) For prayer and sacrifice and expiation.

e) *Supplemented* by a complete system of:

(1) *Schools* for the clergy and laymen of the future.

(2) *Charitable institutions* and hospitals.

II. This side of the Church is the one the average non-Catholic sees and understands. It is, in the eyes of an educated Catholic its least important major claim to fame. **For the Catholic regards his Church:**

A. *Not merely as a group of people* bound together for worship or some other holy purpose. This is true of the Catholic Church but is by no means all. This view is largely Protestant. To the Protestant the churches are groups of congenial people banded together for a common type of worship and religious service.

III. But the **Catholic sees the Church** as:

A. *A divinely commissioned teacher* appointed by Christ to lead men safely and surely to Heaven.

B. *Carrying on the work Christ began* on earth and doing this with His authority:

1. *Speaking with His voice* the same ideas and truths and principles He uttered.

2. *Doing what He commanded* and carrying out the works He began.

3. *Interested in everything* and everyone that interested Him.

4. *Loving the people He loved,* praying for those for whom He prayed, regarding all men as important because He died for them.

C. *The mystical body of Christ.* The Church is the body of which Christ is the Head, the Holy Ghost the soul, and the faithful the members.

Note: This is the doctrine of Christ Himself and of St. Paul. Christ: "I am the vine, you are the branches," etc. (John, XV, 1 ff.) St. Paul: "And He [Christ] is the head of the body, the Church" (Col. I, 18). "Now you are the body of Christ, and members of member" (1 Cor. XII, 27). "And (God) hath made Him head over all the Church which is His body" (Eph. I, 22, 23).

IV. Against this view the **other churches** *are regarded by* **their members:**

    A. *As groups of people* who feel and think more or less alike on matters of religion.

    B. *Gathered to worship God* and make the world better.

    C. Which offer to their followers something *beautiful and satisfying.*

    D. Yet by *no means unquestionably true.*

    E. *Nor very different in one church* from what is offered in another. So that transfer of members from one group to another is relatively easy.

    F. *Without real authority* to command or to compel obedience or acceptance of its teaching or its form of worship.

V. **The Catholic Church presents** to the world and to its followers:

    A. *A definite Leader,* Guide, and Founder, Jesus Christ:

        1. *Who is God* and hence has power:

            a) To claim for Himself *a divine authority* to change the Old Law, to impose a new law, to demand service and acceptance and obedience and worship.

            b) *To establish a Church* to bind men's consciences, to teach a definite doctrine composed of important truths, and to show man the correct way to worship his Creator.

Note: The Divinity of Christ is treated later in the religion course. Here we can indicate only in *briefest outline* the arguments for His divinity:

            c) *Jesus Christ* was a good and sane man (proved by His kindness toward everyone and the wisdom of His doctrines). Yet again and again especially at the solemn moment of His trial:

(1) *When He was questioned by judges* who had a right to ask.

(2) When He was aware that His claim to divinity *would mean His death for blasphemy.*

(3) *He claimed to be God.*

d) Despite this claim (or because of it), *God the Father approved His mission,* His life, and His doctrines by miracles and prophecies that would have misled the people, had He claimed falsely.

e) *He did things only God could dare to do:*

(1) Changed God's law by His own power. Moses, bringing to earth God's law, commanded certain things which Christ by His own authority, changed. "Moses commanded you . . . but I . . .," Christ said repeatedly, changing God's law which Moses never claimed as his own.

(2) Coupled Himself in *equal importance with His Heavenly Father:* "Baptize (that is, make men members of My Church) *in the name of the Father and of the Son."*

(3) Promised of His own power *to send God the Holy Ghost* upon His followers. None but God could command God.

(4) Of His own power *promised eternal reward and eternal punishment;* foretold that He personally would be the judge of the living and the dead; forgave sins; established means of divine communication (grace) with creatures, etc.

(5) Was regarded as God by His followers:

St. John: "In the beginning was the Word, and the Word was with God, and the Word was God." He attributes to Him all power of creation, etc., which God alone could do.

St. Paul: "Christ . . . who is over all things, God blessed forever, Amen" (Rom. IX, 5). And many other places.

(6) He was regarded as God by all His followers, even by heretics, until the days of Arius. And then again by all His followers until relatively modern times.

VI. **This God made man, Jesus Christ, came:**

A. *To lead men safely from earth to heaven.* To give them eternal life, to wipe out their crimes against His Father. "I came that they might have life." For the keeping of the Beatitudes, He promises eternal life. He compares the importance of eternal life to the conquest of the whole world, and stresses eternal life.

B. *To be intercessor between God,* our Father, and His children who had sinned against Him.

    1. This is the constant prayer of Christ.

    2. This is the purpose of His sacrifice upon the cross.

C. *To teach men truth:*

    1. About His Father.

    2. About the Holy Spirit.

    3. About the next world, immortality, eternal joy and eternal loss, right and wrong, His great moral principles.

    4. Christ was preëminently "the teacher," "the master."

D. *To give men a supernatural life,* that is, a life above the merely natural life of food and knowledge and love and the natural knowledge of God.

    1. **Through Grace,** which would enable them to begin on earth a life united with His, and eventually to see God face to face and to love and possess Him eternally.

E. *To console the sorrowful,* care for the weak, comfort those in need. "Come to Me, all ye that labor and are heavily burdened, and I will refresh you."

His numberless miracles of healing and comfort are part of this.

F. *To offer Himself in the Sacrifice of the Cross* and the Sacrifice of the Last Supper as man's victim for sin, thus completing His life of intercession, opening heaven, which had been closed by sin, and bringing men through the darkness of death to life.

VII. **This is the Christ who established the Catholic Church,** a very different Christ from the itinerant preacher of many modern Protestants, the polite, ethical culturist, the teacher of beautiful if somewhat obsolete doctrines.

Problems and Discussions

1. After noting the difference between the Catholic and non-Catholic attitude toward the Church, can you explain why many non-Catholics say that all religions are equally true?

2. Explain to a non-Catholic why this statement of a Protestant business man is only partially and superficially true: "The three greatest

organizations in the world are the Standard Oil Company, the United States Steel Corporation, and the Catholic Church."

3. List some of the elements that make the Catholic Church democratic.
4. Why must the Church be a monarchy? Why can it never become a tyranny?
5. Name some famous Catholics who have throughout history risen from lowly positions to eminence in the Church?
6. Diagram the basic outline of the organization of the Church.
7. In what way does the use of Latin enable the Church to maintain its unity?
8. Explain to a non-Catholic why the Catholic Church is not in the eyes of an educated Catholic merely an organization, but instead:
    a) A devoted and divine teaching authority.
    b) A partaker in Christ's own authority.
    c) The mystical body of Christ.
9. A non-Catholic born a Baptist marries a Presbyterian in a Congregationalist church; later attends Episcopalian services but is satisfied when his children prefer to go to a Methodist Sunday School and later become Christian Scientists. Can his basic attitude toward his church explain this?
10. Indicate briefly to a Unitarian why Christ was really God.
11. Discuss this argument: Since Christ claimed to be God, if He was not God, He was either not a good man or was insane.
12. Why could God the Father simply not allow the marvelous miracles of Christ's life if Christ was not His divine Son?
13. Discuss the common Protestant statement: "Christ came merely to teach us by His example how to live."
14. Explain to a non-Catholic the Catholic position regarding the Church, as far as we have treated it here.
15. Outline the mission of Christ to men.
16. Can you without consulting the next chapter see any similarity between that mission and the mission of the Catholic Church?

Suggested Readings

Note: This list is for Chapters XIII and XIV.

PAMPHLETS

The Queen's Work Press:
    The Church Unconquerable, Dudley.
Loyola University Press:
    Find the Church, Poland, S.J.
The Paulist Press:
    The Direct Route, Kelley.

The Divine Commission of the Church, Harney, C.S.P.
Is One Church as Good as Another? Harney, C.S.P.
Catholic Truth Society:
   How to Look for the True Church, Vaughan, S.J.

BOOKS

Benson, *Christ in the Church* (Herder).

Note: See lists following Chapters XVI to XX, inclusive.

Chapter XIV

THE CHURCH AS CHRIST'S REPRESENTATIVE — II

I. **Christ,** quite aside from His divinity, **was a master with men and thoroughly knew their limitations and needs.**

    A. As God *He wished His work to continue* until the end of time.

    B. As man *He wished this work to be continued by men* chosen to be His partners in establishing and carrying through the Kingdom of His Father.

    C. Christ knew:

        1. That *His life on earth was necessarily limited.*

        2. That *His work* of intercession, sacrifice, guidance, teaching, conferring grace *must continue.*

        3. That *men throughout the ages would need what He had come to give them* and to do for them.

        4. That men follow best *a visible organization* with clearly defined powers and authority.

II. Hence **He established His Church** to carry on His work:

    A. He gathered **His twelve Apostles,** after prayer, thought, and a slow weeding out of those less fitted for the work.

    B. He **trained them** for three years.

    C. He carefully and continuously **talked of His Church** and the work it had to do.

    D. He **gave to the Apostles:**

        1. *A head,* Peter.

        2. His *own power of teaching.* "All power is given to Me in heaven and on earth. Going therefore, teach all nations," etc.

        3. With a *promise that they would never teach incorrectly.* "And the gates of hell shall not prevail against you."

        4. And the *power to open heaven to men;* "I will give thee the keys of the Kingdom of Heaven."

        5. With the *power of sacrifice;* the Mass.

        6. With the *means of grace and the supernatural life.* "Whose sins you shall forgive, they are forgiven." Holy Communion, that is, union with Christ Himself.

The other sacraments.

Prayer: "Ask and you shall receive."

E. This power was given not to them alone but to **their succes-sors** as well.

"I shall be with you all days, even to the consummation of the world."

But as the Apostles were not to live that long, their successors were to see the fulfillment of this promise.

F. Christ would *unite Himself with this Church* and unite them all in Him.

"I am the vine; you are the branches."

"I am the Bridegroom," and hence the Church is the bride.

This is done in the first place through the sacrament of baptism.

III. **The Catholic Church alone claims these powers**, these prerogatives, this absolute certainty of doctrine, and this authority of the keys of the Kingdom of Heaven. But the Catholic Church claims emphatically these powers, and exercises them constantly as it has exercised them since the days of Pentecost.

St. Paul and the early Christians thus regarded the Church as the Spouse of Christ, united with Him, speaking His words, carrying on His work.

IV. Today, as in the beginning, **the Catholic Church speaks the words of Christ,** carries on His work, and regards itself as His **divinely appointed representative.**

A. It consistently claims that *its Founder was divine and hence possessed the right* to establish a Church and endow it with what powers He pleased to give it.

Note: Outside the Catholic Church, the most divergent opinions are held about Jesus Christ, even in groups and churches claiming to be Christian: That He was God, that He was not God, that He suffered hallucinations of greatness, was the world's greatest teacher but made perfectly human mistakes, was the Messias, but not divine, divine but not God, that much of His morality is now outmoded, etc.

The Catholic Church alone speaks of Him consistently, logically, reasonably, and with the certainty of one who knows Him thoroughly.

Like its Founder, the Catholic Church alone speaks "as one having authority."

B. Its intense preoccupation is still that of *saving souls and leading men safely to heaven,* thus accepting Christ's estimate of the relative importance of heaven and of all that the world contains.

Note 1: The Catholic Church is deeply *interested in making earth better and happier;* hence, its defense of the poor and oppressed, and its charity; its stress on the Ten Commandments whose violation is the greatest cause of man's unhappiness and wretchedness.

Note 2: Modern *non-Catholic religions have become more and more "social"* in character, stressing humanitarianism, the need to make a heaven on earth, much concerned with man's social improvement to the exclusion of his eternal destiny.

V. To insure man's gaining of heaven:

A. The Catholic Church stresses the importance of *immortality.*

B. It makes the individual *through Baptism* the child of God and the heir of heaven.

C. It insists on the *importance of the supernatural life,* compared to which every thing on earth is valueless.

D. It asks its religious to show the relative unimportance of earth by making *the three vows,* renouncing self-will, pleasure, and personal property.

E. It keeps before men's eyes the greatness of those heroes, *the saints,* who gave up all for heaven.

F. It constantly recalls *Christ's resurrection* with its guarantee that we too shall rise from the grave.

VI. The Church agrees, against the voice of the modern world, that Christ's *First Commandment is the most important:* "Thou shalt love the Lord thy God with thy whole heart and soul, thy whole mind and thy whole strength."

A. Humanitarianism and much Protestantism insist on the first importance of the love of fellow men. The Catholic Church insists that a man loves his fellow men best and safest when he first loves God.

B. Hence, the Church calls upon men and women to join contemplative orders and spend their lives as Carmelites, Poor Clares, Trappists: (1) Loving God devotedly for the world that does not love Him. (2) Serving Him exclusively through prayer, sacrifice, penance. Through these, the Church carries on the attitude of Christ when He praised Mary who sat at His feet, loving Him, rather than the busy Martha who was working for His comfort.

VII. The Church, as Christ's representative, *regards itself as the inter-cessor* between God and man :

    A. It repeats daily the *Sacrifice of the Cross in the Sacrifice of the Mass*. Christ's eternal priesthood is carried on through His priests.

    B. The *office of the priest,* recited daily, is the Church's official imitation of the ceaseless prayer by which Christ pleaded for the world.

    C. The prayers and sacrifices of its *contemplatives* are offered in intercession for the men and women who do not pray for themselves.

VIII. It still teaches *the same truths* that Christ taught.

Note : Stupidly, the modern world objects to "dogma," forgetting that dogma is merely the unchangeable truths taught us by the divine Christ, and repeated by His representative, the Church. To ask that dogma change is asking Jesus Christ to admit that what He taught the world in order to save it is no longer true, if, indeed, it ever was true.

IX. **The Church teaches, as Christ taught :**

    A. The fatherhood of God.

    B. The brotherhood of man.

    C. The terrible character of sin.

    D. That after death are judgment, heaven, and hell.

    E. That the Holy Ghost indwells in the Christian.

    F. That grace and the supernatural life are of supreme impor-tance.

    G. The communion of saints.

    H. The power of prayer.

    I. The great moral law regarding :

        1. Purity.

        2. Honesty.

        3. Poverty of spirit.

        4. Respect for the poor.

        5. The Beatitudes.

    J. The importance of Holy Communion.

    K. The fact that sins can be forgiven.

X. It gives **grace to men through the means** which Christ used and left to His Church :

    A. *Baptism,* with its "new birth" to a new life that Christ described to Nicodemus as essential, and its incorporation of the Christian into the Mystical Body of Christ.

B. *Confirmation,* with its gift of the Holy Ghost, promised to the Apostles.

C. *Holy Communion,* which was to be done in commemoration of Christ.

D. *Penance and Confession,* with the forgiveness of sins, a power granted to the Apostles and their successors.

E. *Matrimony,* with its grace to help the young couple carry through life their important responsibilities.

F. *Holy Orders,* with its transmission of the apostolic powers to the successors of the Apostles.

G. *Extreme unction,* with its strengthening of the sick for their final struggle and entrance into God's presence.

XI. Hence, the Church is not merely an institution, nor an organization, nor a body of people gathered together, but it is **Christ's divinely appointed representative** carrying on His work in the world:

A. Demanding to be heard.

B. Promising heaven to those who follow.

C. Serving man with the same love and zeal that characterized the Savior.

Problems and Discussions

1. If the various churches and denominations contradict one another (as they certainly do) can they all be the true Church of Christ?

2. Discuss this statement: Christ, as a farsighted man who knew human nature, was bound to establish an infallible teacher to guide the human race and carry on His work.

3. Show to a non-Catholic that Christ established such a teacher and guide.

4. What qualities would a man who simply read the story of Christ's establishment of His Church expect to find in it?

5. What effect has the "war of the sects" upon the man who is thinking about becoming a Christian?

6. Would you agree with this statement: Outside the Catholic Church today, almost no one knows Jesus Christ?

7. Show in parallel columns that the work and mission and teachings of Christ are actually being carried on in the Catholic Church.

8. Answer a non-Catholic who says: "The main function of religion is to make a man happier in this life."

9. But will the religion that is truly Christ's also serve to make a man happier in this life?
10. Show why the Church of Christ should be and should act as:
    a) An infallible teacher.
    b) A sure guide to eternity.
    c) An intercessor between God and men.
    d) Treasurer of divine grace.
    e) Comforter of the afflicted.
11. Discuss the common statement: "I love religion but I dislike dogma."
12. Mention some of the moral doctrines and principles taught by Christ that are still being taught by the Church though largely forgotten by the world outside the Church.
13. In parallel columns show how the natural life of man is cared for and supported by the action of the sacraments.
14. Explain to a non-Catholic precisely how the Catholic feels about the Catholic Church in gratitude for what it does for him.

Chapter XV

GREAT CATHOLICS

I. Owing to the fact that **Catholics in America live:**
  A. In a *predominantly non-Catholic country:*
  B. With wealth and power largely *in non-Catholic hands.*
  C. And are in many cases *descendants of races and nations* in which:
    1. As in England, Ireland, Scotland, parts of Germany, *education* and the learned professions *were denied to Catholics* by force of penal law.
    2. As in France, Italy, Mexico, Portugal, the Church was *not allowed to operate its school system,* and power was largely in Masonic hands:
  D. American Catholics sometimes feel that non-Catholic religions or non-religious groups produce more great men than does the Catholic faith.
  E. They grow apologetic about their fellow Catholics.

II. Yet, while the American *Who's Who* may be predominantly non-Catholic (since America itself is predominantly non-Catholic), the World's *Who's Who* and the *Who's Who* of history is overwhelmingly Catholic.

III. In general, it is a **difficult task to list** really great men and women:
  A. *True greatness is hard to appraise.* Luck, opportunity, the particular needs of a particular period of history may dominate a person and thrust apparent greatness upon them.

If Ferdinand and Isabella had been defeated at Granada, Columbus would not have been given the opportunity to discover the new world. U. S. Grant was almost a nonentity until the Civil War gave him his chance.

The invention of the microscope made possible the achievements of successive scientists who might have been unknown had they lived before its invention.

  B. *God's idea of greatness may not often be man's idea.* Man judges only by external success and actual achievement. Thus a devoted mother quite unknown to the public may be greater than the world's most famous actress or woman leader. An honest grocer's clerk may be more important than a world conqueror.

C. *Often the world's truly great live in deliberate secrecy.* The architects who built the great Cathedrals left no record of their identity. Great monks and nuns changed their names to escape fame.

D. *To be regarded as great by the Catholic Church,* a man must not only have been born a Catholic, he must die in the Catholic faith. Thus Voltaire was born a Catholic; so were Luther, Photius, Henry VIII, Renan; Rousseau was for a time a nominal Catholic; but they are not Catholics because they died out of the Church.

E. The *Church is not primarily interested in fostering successful or brilliant men.* It is interested in caring for and developing good men. Hence, its first and exclusive claim is that it is the Mother of Saints; that is, of men and women who were both great and good.

Note 1: A saint may be a person who was personally great, but publicly inconspicuous. Most frequently, saints are conspicuous for their achievements as well as for their personal holiness.

Note 2: The Catholic Church is unique in its claim to possessing saints; i.e., men and women of heroic goodness and greatness. Whatever "saints" are claimed by the Protestant churches are all Catholic. Since the reformation, only the Catholic Church has given the world new saints. Once only in recent times did the Greek Orthodox Church claim to canonize.

Thus: The four outstanding leaders honored by the Anglican (Episcopalian) Church with statues over the entrance of Westminster are:

1. St. Augustine, a Catholic bishop, sent by Pope Gregory the Great to convert England.
2. St. Dunstan, a Catholic created bishop by the Pope.
3. St. Thomas à Becket, a Catholic archbishop, who fought an English king trying to do less than Henry VIII later accomplished.
4. Cranmer, a Protestant, not a saint, and of decidedly questionable life.

IV. **Catholic saints are often the great national heroes:**
    A. St. Edward the Confessor of England.
    B. St. Louis and St. Joan of Arc, in France.

C. St. Stanislaus and St. Wenceslaus, in Poland.

D. St. Stephen, of Hungary.

Note: Today Protestants continue to worship in churches dedicated to Catholic saints: e.g., Irish Protestants in St. Patrick's Cathedral; German Protestants in churches dedicated to St. Boniface; Scandinavian Protestants in St. Olaf's Cathedral.

V. **Saints** have often been **magnificent leaders** of world movements, great figures in history even if they had not been canonized.

A. *St. Benedict:* father of monasticism: who, with his monks:

1. *Saved the pagan culture* from barbaric annihilation.

2. Converted large parts of the world to Christianity and civilization. (Benedictine monks were the great missionaries to England, Ireland, Germany, Saxony, the Far North.)

3. *Built the strongholds of art and education* from which came modern European culture.

B. *Great sainted popes* were dominant figures of history:

1. *St. Gregory the Great* was the outstanding man of his century.

2. *St. Gregory VII* (Hildebrand), fought against the absolutism of the Emperors.

3. *St. Sylvester* was the spiritual father of Constantine.

4. *St. Pius V* was the leading figure of the Counter Reformation, and largely responsible for saving Europe from the Turkish invasion.

C. *St. Francis of Assisi,* beloved of all artists, Catholics, and non-Catholics alike, was:

1. *The founder of the Franciscans,* whose work is world wide.

2. *The father of the Catholic Renaissance,* inspirer of untold poetry and painting and music.

3. *The most Christlike figure* in a thousand years.

D. *St. Camillus of Lellis,* is the *father of the Red Cross.*

E. *St. Vincent de Paul* is the inspiration and organizer of *modern charity,* and the founder of religious orders carrying on this charitable work throughout the world.

F. *St. Ignatius of Loyola,* was one of the main factors in the *Counter Reformation,* founder of modern educational methods, and father of the teaching order, the Jesuits.

G. *St. Catherine of Siena,* called by non-Catholic historians *the greatest woman in all modern history,* changed the course of Italian history, restored the Pope from Avignon to Rome, and dominated her day.

H. *St. Joan of Arc,* the great heroine of France and womanhood, was the outstanding figure of her day and one of the most fascinating figures of all time.

I. *St. Theresa of Avila,* restored the great Carmelite order throughout the world.

VI. **Saints have come from every class of society;** for example: St. Isidore, the farmer; St. Zita, the cook; Blessed Bernadette, the shepherdess; St. Sebastian, the soldier; St. Hugh of Lincoln, the small boy; St. Agnes, the young girl; St. Pancratius, the boy in his 'teens; St. Philomene, the girl in her 'teens; St. Yves, the lawyer; St. Luke, the physician; St. Thomas Aquinas, the writer; St. Albert the Great, the teacher; St. Louis, St. Edward, kings; St. Elizabeth of Hungary, St. Margaret of Scotland, queens; St. Frances of Rome, a noble mother and widow; St. Alphonsus Rodriguez, a married tradesman afterwards a lay brother; and so through all the walks of life and all the professions.

VII. Only a small percentage of the great and good have been canonized. For 1500 years, **practically every great name in Europe was Catholic,** and the great achievements that turned wandering tribes into modern Europe were the work of Catholic leaders, pioneers, thinkers, philosophers, statesmen, generals.

VIII. **The great kings** of whom European countries are proud were Catholic:

A. Constantine and Justinian; Clovis, Charles Martel, Charlemagne.

B. The heroes of whom England is particularly proud: Harold; William the Conqueror; The Black Prince; Richard the Lion-Hearted; Henry V.

C. The great crusading kings of every land.

D. The Norman kings who rebuilt Europe and gave it its vigor and manly characteristics.

E. Ferdinand and Isabella, final conquerors of the Moors and the liberators of Spain.

IX. **The rulers and illustrious statesmen** were all Catholic:

A. The chancellors of European nations were usually archbishops. Stephen Langton, Catholic archbishop, won the Magna Charta for England.

B. Don John, of Austria, saved Europe at the Battle of Lepanto.

C. Catholics molded modern England, France, Spain, Portugal, Scandinavia, and gave Europe its parliamentary form of government.

X. **The great pioneers** of modern European civilization were Catholic:

A. Caxton gave the world *the printing press*.

B. Marco Polo set the standard for all *explorers*.

C. Erasmus and Dean Colet fostered *modern education*.

D. Henry VII was the father of the *English Navy*.

XI. **European literature**, in language and forms, takes its rise from Catholic sources; for example:

A. Caedmon is the father of English poetry.

B. Chaucer is the father of modern English.

C. Langland is the father of English prose.

D. Dante is the father and inspiration of Italian poetry, and "the morning star of the Renaissance."

E. Petrarch is the great poet of the Italian Renaissance.

F. The Troubadours established French poetry.

G. Moliere is the father of modern drama.

H. Cervantes is the founder of the modern novel.

I. Calderon is, with Shakespeare, the father of the modern stage.

XII. **In philosophy:**

A. Catholic philosophers rediscovered for Europe the philosophy of Plato and Aristotle.

B. Albert the Great, Thomas Aquinas and their associates established Scholastic philosophy.

C. Descartes, greatest of mathematicians, was the founder of much modern philosophy (with which, however, Catholics disagree).

XIII. **The contribution of Catholics to science** would need several volumes: Names only can be suggested for further investigation: Copernicus, Mendel, Ampère, Volta, Roger Bacon, the reformers of the calendar, Galileo, Kirscher, Lamarck, Marconi, Pasteur, Ricci, Roentgen, and scores of others.

Under the list of scientists should be put the **world explorers** who opened a new world to civilization: Columbus, Magellan, the Cabots, Balboa, and their Catholic followers.

XIV. If the **Catholic painters** were to be eliminated from history, most of the world's greatest art would be instantly destroyed. Starting from the founders of modern painting, Giotto and Cimabue, and working back through the mosaics of the Middle Ages or forward through the Renaissance, art is in Catholic hands: Fra Angelico, Raphael, Michelangelo, Titian, Valesquez, Rembrandt, Rubens, and many others.

XV. The same is almost equally true of **music,** which got its modern notation and form from the monks, and was carried to perfection by Catholic composers; through Palestrina, Haydn, Beethoven, Verdi, Puccini, and many others.

XVI. Deliberately this **chapter has been shortened** to prevent its seeming a catalog. The student should note:

A. That hundreds of thousands of the **world's greatest martyrs** are not even known by name; e.g., the martyrs of the Roman persecutions, the Japanese persecutions, the men and women who suffered under Henry and Elizabeth in England.

B. That among the world's greatest are its **unknown mothers and fathers,** whose place is sure with God, whose mark and influence on the world cannot be estimated, but who will be unrecognized until the Last Judgment.

C. That Catholics have often been singularly **disdainful of fame.** Thus we do not know:

1. Who built the cathedrals.

2. Who made the medieval manuscripts of vestments or metal work.

3. Who composed the songs of the troubadours.

4. Who actually composed most of the Gregorian music.

5. Who perfected Romanesque, Norman, and Gothic architecture.

6. Who designed and invented stained glass.

7. Who established the trade routes of Europe and Asia.

D. That for 1,500 years there was **no Protestantism to claim a single great man or woman** or a single great achievement of European history. During that time was written the great *Who's Who* of world history.

E. Since the Reformation, wherever Catholicity has not been hopelessly hampered (as in England, Ireland, Mexico) by laws making Catholic education impossible; or where the Catholic religion itself was not absolutely banned (as in Scandinavia) ; or where persecution (as in France, Spain, Portugal, Russia, the Netherlands) has not continuously or intermittently raged; Catholics have given their full share of great men and women to the public life of the nation.

Problems and Discussions

1. From what educational, financial, and social disadvantages have Catholics labored in America?
2. Judging the Church from the standards set by Christ, would you expect it to be more interested in good men or famous men? Why?
3. Can you say that the world's famous men have often also been the world's great rogues?
4. Define true greatness: in the eyes of a just man; in the eyes of God.
5. Why are the great often unknown?
6. Is there a connection between the fact that Christ's Church must be holy and the exclusive possession of saints by the Catholic Church?
7. Discussion: The saints as a group made the greatest contribution to the happiness and forward movement of the world.
8. Could you explain to a non-Catholic why membership in the Catholic Church is the most distinguished in the world?
9. Explain the Catholic differences between the American *Who's Who* and the *Who's Who* of history.
10. Though the following died Catholics, why are they not listed among the Church's boasted members: Napoleon, Montaigne, Oscar Wilde, Fra Lippo Lippi, Lorenzo de Medici, Charles II of England?
11. Give instances from history where chance or opportunity was the factor that brought greatness to light.
12. Could you explain why so many great Catholics have been, apparently with deliberation, careless about fame?
13. Why can it be said that no class of society has failed to give the Church its saints? Illustrate, using names different from those in the chapter.
14. Can it be said that the saints made Europe Christian before Christianity made it modern?
15. List some famous Catholic statesmen; pioneers of civilization; men of literature.
16. For what were the scientists mentioned in the chapter famous? Add some others from your own knowledge.

17. Discuss this statement: Catholic painters have filled the world with its greatest artistic beauty.
18. Show that the history of music is predominantly Catholic.
19. Answer a non-Catholic who says: "The Catholic Church is the Church of the poor, ignorant, and nondescript."
20. Discussion: Is the Catholic population of the present giving the world its fair share of great men and women? Explain.

Suggested Readings

PAMPHLETS

The Queen's Work Press:
  The White Plume of Aloysius, Barrett, S.J.
  A Short Life in the Saddle, Barrett, S.J.
America Press:
  An Outlaw of Christ (Father Pro).
  St. Joan of Arc, Reville, S.J.
  St. Margaret Mary, Reville, S.J.
The Paulist Press:
  St. Elizabeth of Hungary, Riley.
  St. Francis of Assisi, Ross.
  St. Francis Xavier, Phillips.
  St. Gabriel, Passionist, Lummer.
Catholic Truth Society:
  Father Damien, Denis.
  Mother Phillipine Duchesne.
  St. Vincent de Paul, Martindale, S.J.

BOOKS

Windle, *Twelve Catholic Men of Science* (Catholic Truth Society).
Walsh, *Catholic Churchmen in Science* (American Ecclesiastical Review).
Zahm, *Catholic Science and Catholic Scientists* (Kilner).
Kneller, *Christianity and the Leaders of Modern Science* (Herder).
Gheon, *The Secret of the Cure D'Ars* (Sheed and Ward).
Morton, *Sobieski* (Eyre and Spottiswodde).
Morton, *The Irish Way,* Short Lives of Irish Saints (Sheed & Ward).
Morton, *The English Way,* Short Lives of English Saints (Sheed and Ward).
Blunt, *Great Wives and Mothers* (Devin-Adair).
Papini, *Laborers in the Vineyard* (Sheed and Ward).
Sadlier, *Names that Live in Catholic Hearts* (Benziger).
Brégy, *Poets and Pilgrims* (Benziger).
Martindale, *Catholic Thought and Thinkers* (Harding and More).

Chapter XVI

THE CATHOLIC FAITH AS A WORKING SYSTEM OF LIFE

I. **Life is either a "meaningless jumble of unrelated events"** or it is **a series of related parts, with**

    A. *An objective,* some place toward which a man progresses through life; some purpose that makes life significant.

    B. *A reason for man's existence;* so that a man is not merely a final accident in a series of accidents, but the result of a plan of which he is an intended part.

    C. *An explanation of the questions* a man asks of life:

        1. Why has it been given me?

        2. What am I to do with it?

        3. Where will it lead me?

        4. Has it a purpose that I can understand and help fulfill?

II. **Science, philosophy, and religion,** no matter on what else they disagree, have each tried to explain life, to solve its purpose, to answer the questions a man asks of it.

    A. *A thousand different theories* have been advanced, each endeavoring to explain life. No two have agreed in more than a few points.

        1. *The Hindu* sees life as an advancement by stages of development until final absorption in divinity, without ultimate consciousness of self: the eternal oblivion called Nirvana.

        2. *The Mohammedan* sees life as ruled by inexorable fate that determines a man's destiny, and the crown and goal of life and unending Paradise of purely sensual delights.

        3. *The Agnostic Philosopher* admits he has no answer to the principal questions of life. He knows nothing of God, life after death, and ultimate objective for life, life's real purposes. He does not know whether life has a meaning and believes that no one can ever know.

        4. *The Materialistic Philosopher* sees man as one of the major accidents of the universe, made up of chemical elements and

physical forces, destined to disintegration and a return into constituent elements. There is no God, no free will, no souls, no destiny beyond this visible earth.

5. *The Pantheist* sees that all things are God and that men are parts of God. For a time man is apparently separated from God but his destiny is to return to God.

6. *The Scientific Monist,* following in the footsteps of Haeckel, acknowledges nothing except matter and force, out of which all things are supposed to have been evolved. He gives to matter attributes that belong to God alone, infinity, eternity, etc., and makes all things, intellectual and spiritual, identical with matter. Philosophically there is a materialistic and an idealistic monism. Matter is the sole reality acknowledged by the one, and mind the sole reality accepted by the other.

7. *The Atheist,* who is the materialist *par excellence,* claims that the world has no creator, that man has no Father who is in heaven, that all life is the result of accident, that man himself is a purposeless being in a purposeless world.

8. *The Hedonist* claims that the purpose of life is pleasure. The sensual Hedonist makes this to consist in a purely sensual gratification. The higher type of Hedonist makes this the enjoyment of the arts, culture, intellectual life.

9. *The Stoic,* regards duty as the purpose of life, usually a duty which the individual imposes upon himself.

III. Contrary to the belief of those who read the Sunday supplements, *science does not in general give or attempt to give any explanation* of why life is or what it is meant to be used for. It only attempts to *explain what makes up the individual elements of life* and shows how they act upon one another.

A. It explains the *chemical and physical constituents* of material objects.

B. It seeks to trace the *development of animals* we now possess from their more remote ancestors.

C. It studies the *actions of men and animals* and endeavors to explain their motives, their consequences, their origins.

D. It analyzes the *relationships of one group* of beings to another; e.g., the relation of chemicals, of stars, of one type of animal to another, etc.

1. In seeking to explain these relationships it develops **theories:**

a) *The Theory of Gravity:* To explain why all material objects are attracted to one another.

b) *The Theory of Evolution:* To explain how the present world developed with its animals, plants, chemicals, into the form it now holds.

c) *The Theory of Ether:* to explain how light and electricity travel through space.

d) *The Nebular Theory or Hypothesis:* To explain the origin of the stars and solar systems.

e) And a hundred other theories.

IV. **None of these theories,** religious, philosophical, or scientific, **can explain life** satisfactorily or completely. They will be discussed at length in philosophy and science classes and in religion courses. The Catholic Faith is not a theory, but we may regard it here as a working system which explains life satisfactorily.

Note: A theory is always proposed without actual proof. If ever it can be proved, it forthwith ceases to be a theory and becomes a fact, a certainty. A theory is simply an explanation that actually fits a series of facts and makes them clear whether in itself it be true or not. Thus no one has ever explained or proved the existence of ether. It may or may not exist. We do not know. But the theory of a universal ether explains light, electricity, facts like radio, the interaction of star on star; so it is accepted because it explains the case.

V. While the Catholic Faith, therefore, is not a theory, and will later in the course, be fully proved, it may yet for the present be similarly treated as a working system that explains the essential facts of life, and that is:

A. *Logical:* Every step follows from the step that preceded it.

B. *Satisfactory to the heart of man:* Once a man sees it completely, he admits it best explains the facts of life and seems right and proper.

C. *Fitting in with the facts as man finds them:* The Catholic Faith accepts the existing facts and puts them together into a unified and comprehensive whole.

D. *Dignified:* It gives man his proper dignity and places him in a noble relationship to the rest of the world.

E. *Provable and actually proved:* It can be demonstrated by arguments the value of which has never been shaken. It is thus established as a fact and not a theory.

F. These proofs are given throughout the religion, philosophy, and scientific courses.

Hence, we here offer *the Catholic Faith as a working system by which life can be explained completely, beautifully, and in accord with all the facts.*

VI. The Catholic Working System of Life:

A. Whence Life?

1. Life is *not an accident*.

a) Accidents result, as universal experience shows, in ruins, things less perfect than the constituents of the accident.

b) Or when they do occasionally result in something fine, when an experimenter accidentally stumbles on a discovery, they do not repeat themselves consistently. If they do repeat, they cease to be accidents.

c) Hence: (1) So complicated a thing as the universe could not be caused by accidents nor kept in existence by accidents.

(2) So wonderful a thing as the human body or the human mind could be even less an accident.

(3) Accidents do not keep recurring regularly; but the universe keeps on regularly, with everything from seasons to the rotation of complete solar systems; and individuals regularly reproduce others of their kind.

(4) Accidents are the absence of law; life is the fulfillment of a magnificent series of laws.

VII. Life is *something given by a Being* above and beyond the world.

Note: No one can give himself what he has not got. No man until he exists can give life, and then cannot give it to himself. If life did not exist in the universe, as scientists assert of the past, the universe could not give itself life. If it did exist, it must have come from outside the universe, since nothing can give itself what it has not got, in this case, life.

If life began by a combination of elements:

1. These elements must have got their existence from some power outside themselves.

2. The proper combination of these elements gives evidence of plan and law, which requires a planner and lawgiver.

A. **This Being gave man life:**
1. *That was like His own:*
   a) With the *power of knowing;* the Being must have known before He could create.
   b) With the *power of loving;* the Being must have wanted the creatures He created, and wanting and loving are synonyms.
   c) With the *power of calling other beings into existence.*
So man produces others of his own kind; the arts, crafts, literature, etc.
2. Since plan runs through the whole universe, and all things have a purpose which they serve, this Being must have given men, the most important creatures, *a plan and purpose in their lives.*
3. Hence, **life is a gift from a Superior Being.**
4. Hence, too, **life must have a purpose;** otherwise in the sole instance of man, the Superior Being would have acted without reason.

VIII. What is the Purpose of Life?

A. *It is a period of trial during which, by proving that one can use life well, one deserves a fuller and more perfect life.*

Men are never satisfied with this life and what it gives them. The more they get of earth, the more discontented they are. World conquerors sigh for new worlds to conquer; the taste of riches, power, pleasure simply creates an insatiable appetite for more.

Yet, all men dream of perfect happiness that they never attain.

B. Hence, this *life is a period of probation* during which men prove their worth:
1. For this they need and actually have *the freedom and power to choose right or wrong,* good or evil.
2. *If they choose good,* they use life well, help their fellow men and improve the world. For this *they deserve a fuller and finer life.*
3. *If they choose evil,* they use life badly, harm their fellow men, and try to spoil the world. For this *they deserve to be deprived of a fuller and more perfect life.*

The only possible explanation of life with its trials, its problems, its unsatisfactory character, its sense of incompleteness; the fact that it is ended before man has exhausted or begun to exhaust its possibilities, its beauties, actualities, experiences; the fact that one is constantly forced to make decisions between right and wrong, between what hurts or improves oneself, others, the world at large, is this:

Our life on earth is a prelude to another world. It is the testing ground for another life. Its purpose is to give men time and opportunity to prove their value and their worth.

IX. How Shall Men Use This Life?

    A. Men left to themselves agree on a great many things; *the vast majority agree* and always have agreed:

        1. That there is a *Supreme Being* who has established this world and rewards or punishes its right or wrong use.

        2. That there is *a life beyond this life* which is the fulfillment of this present life, its adequate reward or its merited punishment.

        3. That there are *things positively wrong and things positively right*.

    B. But they have *disagreed* on a great many things of vast importance:

        1. About *the nature of the Supreme Being* or Beings.

        2. About the *character of this life* beyond this present life.

        3. About *what is right* and *what is wrong* in many cases.

X. Hence, the **Supreme Being could not leave men** in these perplexities but must help them to certainty about these important facts. To insure this:

    A. He implanted *a natural religious inclination* in all human beings. No nation has failed to show signs of this instinct. People lose it only after tremendous effort.

    B. He gave men the mental ability *to rise from the visible world to some knowledge of the invisible;* and to gain from creatures a knowledge of their Creator. Even the pagan philosophers possessed and exercised this power.

    C. He sent His *chosen religious leaders* to explain life and man's relationship to this life and the next. These were the patriarchs and prophets of the Old Law.

    D. He sent His *only-begotten Son* to live this life perfectly as an example for mankind. This was Jesus Christ, the Messias.

    E. He gave mankind *an infallible Church* to:

        1. Teach men to live correctly.

        2. Help them with important strength.

XI. Whither Does This Life Tend?

A. Since the Supreme Being created life and gave it to man, He must have had a purpose worthy of Himself. Such a purpose could only be connected with Himself, though at the same time connected with the happiness of His creatures.

B. So He makes as the *objective of this present life* **a fuller and more perfect life** patterned on His own, in which:

1. *Men will be with this Supreme Being forever.*

2. *They will know Him,* and through Him, *the truths* that the human mind has struggled to know.

3. *They will love Him,* and through Him *all the beautiful* and worthy things of the universe.

XII. How Is This Fuller Life Possible?

A. In order to make possible this fuller and more perfect life, which is like His own life, in that it possesses Him, knows Him, loves Him, and experiences perfect happiness, the Supreme Being **elevated man and endowed him with powers and possibilities beyond what his nature demanded:**

1. The power *to see the Supreme Being face to face* in the life to come.

2. The power *to become His adopted sons* and heirs of His kingdom.

3. The power *to share His life* now and in eternity.

a) This power is precisely the thing promised by Christ, the Son of God, and called Grace.

XIII. What Did Man Do With Life?

A. Every man feels in his nature **a strange war:**

1. *He approves* and knows he should do what is good and right and noble.

2. *He is torn from the* good by terrific impulses (called disordered passion) toward things which he knows to be base and low and evil.

a) This came about because:

(1) *Man's ancestor threw away the special powers* that God had added to his nature. And, like a wasteful ancestor, what he flung away, his children no longer had the right to claim.

(2) *This ancestor voluntarily turned toward evil,* and

left his children with his inherited inclination toward evil.

B. Man has *to be left free* so that he can, by his free choice between the good and evil use of life, prove his right to the fuller life.

    1. Man, left free, allows himself to *prefer the selfish moment of self-gratification,* power, wealth, pride, even though he knows this is harming others as well as himself and is opposed to unselfishness and the service of others. This forms **habits** that incline the man toward evil.

    2. On the contrary, men who live unselfishly, heroically, with due regard for the rights of the Supreme Being and of their fellow men, *grow strong in their power to choose right.* They are developing this present life and meriting the future life.

XIV. **What Value Has Life?**

    A. A value that is measured by the purpose contained in it: The enjoyment of eternal happiness and the complete realization of one's own faculties in company with a Supreme Being of perfect truth and beauty.

    B. Hence all *other happiness* of earth:

        1. *If it leads a man toward* this destiny, is good.

        2. *If it leads a man away* from this ultimate purpose, is not only *wrong* but terribly stupid, as lust is stupid, or the love of wealth.

        3. *If it neither helps nor hinders* a man to improve this life, it is *indifferent.*

XV. Hence, summarized: **The Catholic Working System of Life** is this:

    A. Man is important because a Supreme Being thought it worth His while to bring him into existence.

    B. Life is precious because:

        1. It comes as a gift from a Supreme Being.

        2. It is given in order to be used to win a higher life.

    C. Men are free to use or abuse this life, and by so doing to help themselves and others or harm themselves or others.

    D. If men use it well, they merit a life beyond this life, finer, fuller, and more perfect.

    E. If they use it badly, they deserve to lose forever the life beyond life.

F. The Supreme Being has added to such natural happiness as men could deserve by the right use of life, the power to enjoy a life like His own.

G. He has given men guides to show them how to live.

H. And helps to assist and strengthen them in their difficulties.

I. But men have deliberately turned to evil, with sad consequences to themselves and their descendants.

J. The Supreme Being, despite this, still continues to help men to attain the purpose of life.

K. Hence, life is full of meaning, of beauty, and of high purpose.

L. Hence, a man knows why he exists, what purpose he can find in life.

M. Hence, he knows too what to do and what to avoid.

N. In fine, he has a working system that not only explains life but explains how to regulate his personal conduct in relation to the purposes of life. Best of all, it is a working system which is not a theory, like evolution, but a fact, a certainty.

Problems and Discussions

1. Have you in reading modern literature noted a tendency to regard life as a "meaningless jumble of unrelated events"?

2. Show that it is incredible that in the midst of a perfectly ordered universe, man should be without purpose and destiny.

3. What modern examples have you met in life or in reading of the various theories mentioned?

4. Discuss this statement: "The modern unbeliever is usually a Hedonist."

5. Briefly analyzing the false theories given, show one way in which each:
   a) Is against the common facts of experience.
   b) Lowers the dignity of mankind.

6. If the theory of materialistic evolution denies man's immortality, soul, and free will and excludes a Supreme Being, show that it:
   a) Is against the common facts of experience.
   b) Lowers the dignity of mankind.

7. Explain to a non-Catholic why you think life needs a theory to explain it.

8. Discuss this statement: The Catholic working system of life while admitting a Supreme Being, is deeply concerned about the dignity of mankind.

9. Explain to a non-Catholic, what the Catholic viewpoint holds about the origin of life. Does this explain the facts?

10. Discuss this frequent modern statement: "Man is just the supreme accident of an unplanned world."
11. What qualities could you argue are possessed by the Supreme Being who created the universe and man?
12. In parallel columns place the qualities that the Supreme Being possessed and passed on to His creatures.
13. Explain to a non-Catholic the ultimate purpose of life. Why does this purpose demand that men have free wills?
14. If men are destined for supreme happiness, how does it happen that they find themselves so severely tempted to sin?
15. Without using the word *grace*, explain to a non-Catholic what its place is in the Catholic working system of life.
16. Discuss this statement: "I should be terribly bored with the future life promised to Christians."
17. Answer the man who says: "Life is valueless and I am sorry I was born."
18. Do you find any of the essential facts that are not explained by the Catholic working system of life?

Suggested Readings

PAMPHLETS

The Queen's Work Press:
Has Life Any Meaning? Lord, S.J.
When Sorrow Comes, Lord, S.J.
God and the Depression, Lord, S.J.
Random Shots, Lord, S.J.
Truth's the Thing, Lord, S.J.
Revolt Against Heaven, Lord, S.J.
The Catholic Truth Society:
The Beginning and End of Man, Knox.

BOOKS

Dudley, *The Shadow on the Earth* (Longmans).
Chesterton, *Orthodoxy* (Dodd).
Chesterton, *The Everlasting Man,* First Part (Dodd).
Chesterton, *The Thing* (Sheed and Ward).
Chesterton, *The Catholic Church and Conversion* (Macmillan).
Connolly, *Mr. Blue* (Macmillan).
Williams, *Catholicism and the Catholic Mind* (Dial Press).
Williams, *Why I am a Catholic* by Belloc, Knox, Goodier, Kaye-Smith (Burns & Oates).
Belloc, *The Question and the Answer* (Bruce).

Chapter XVII

THE DEVOTIONAL LIFE OF THE CHURCH

I. **Devotion** is often confused in the popular mind with weakly sentimental religious emotionalism, effeminate "religiosity." This is absolutely wrong.

    A. **Devoted** is from the word, *devoveo* which implies one bound by a solemn word, a pledge made out of deep loyalty and desire to do something hard and splendid because of a belief in a cause or the love of a person.

        1. A man shows his *devotion to his country* by fighting and dying for it.

        2. A woman shows her *devotion to her husband and children* by the beauty and orderliness of her house, and its peace and happiness.

        3. A man of fine characteristics will be *devoted to his friends,* showing them sympathy, a spirit of coöperation, of generosity, of loyalty in their time of need.

    B. So **devotion** is a word properly associated with the *finest instincts of life:*

        1. Devotion to duty, to art, to a career, to wife and children, to the good of humanity, to the spread of truth, to justice, etc.

    C. These natural "devotions" are *expressed in outward signs.*

Note: Man is a creature of body and soul, of emotions and intellect; hence, instinctively and necessarily he expresses outwardly through bodily gestures and emotional reactions what he thinks or feels deeply and intensely.

        1. Thus *devotion to country* is shown:

          a) In the *salute* to the flag.

          b) In tributes paid to the *tomb* of the unknown soldier.

          c) In patriotic *parades.*

        Which are merely the external but inevitable expression of a love for and belief in a country.

        2. *Devotion to wife and children* is shown:

          a) In external signs of *personal affection.*

          b) In *gifts* of flowers and similar things.

          c) In acts of *personal service.*

    d) In a spirit of *home building*.

  3. *Devotion to art or science* is shown:

    a) In the *erection* of theaters, art museums, museums of science.

    b) In an interest in and support of *scientists and artists*.

    c) In *applause* given to fine pieces of work.

    d) In the *presentation of awards*, medals, prizes, cups, etc.

  4. When a man really believes a person or thinks of him as important enough to win his approval, he shows this. devotion externally:

    a) In service.

    b) In personal sacrifice for the sake of the person or thing.

    c) In some sort of emotional display.

  5. Frequently this interest in a person and belief in him takes the form of sincerest flattery called *imitation*.

  All this comes under the general term, devotion.

II. The Catholic Church realizes that:

A. *God the Father* is a person who can *inspire the highest type of gratitude* and love and devotion and loyalty.

B. *Jesus Christ* is a person who will awaken *the eager acceptance and heroic devotion* of men and women who come to know Him.

C. *The saints* awaken a response to their *heroism and a desire to imitate* and follow them.

D. *The truths and beauties of the Catholic Faith* inspire man with responsive emotions that must express themselves externally.

III. Hence, the Church has developed:

A. Beautiful ways by which *to show man's gratitude to God* the Father, and his consequent loyalty.

B. Methods of stimulating and developing man's *willing companionship with Christ*, the Leader.

C. Means of *honoring the saints* and learning better to follow their heroic example.

D. The most satisfactory forms in which man's *religious emotion and convictions* can be expressed — his emotions of:

  1. *Love* of God and His saints.

  2. *Sorrow* for sin and fear of its consequences.

  3. *Reverence* for the Creator.

  4. *Loyalty* to the Kingdom of Christ.

  5. *Happiness* in the certainties of faith.

IV. This devotional life of the Church is:
  A. Eminently *natural* in its appeal to men.

Note: Even men who do not accept Catholic truth realize the wisdom of Catholic religious practice, comparing the beautiful and appealing worship of the Catholic Church with the cold and unappealing services of non-Catholic groups.

  B. *Varied* to meet all temperaments, all classes, ages, groups.
    1. As *intellectual* as a closed retreat where a man faces the truths of life and eternity, and measures his own life and conduct in terms of eternal principles.
    2. As *emotional* as a passion sermon, in which, however, emotion is based solidly on facts and proved truths.
    3. *Requiring deep knowledge and study,* as for a full knowledge of the Mass and its significance.
    4. *Requiring only simple faith and love,* as for a procession of the Blessed Sacrament or the use of the rosary.
  C. *Permitting a man to exercise* his natural emotional life.
    1. The *crucifix* corresponds to the flag of a country.
    2. The *church building* is the external expression of the important worship it houses.
    3. The beauty of *vestment* and altar furnishings give God the best products of the arts.
    4. *United prayer* associates him with his fellow men and gives him a sense of strength and union.
    5. The glory of *ritual,* the ceremonies of Mass, Benediction, Vespers, Tenebræ, processions, etc., satisfy his deeply esthetic nature.
    6. The varying emotional ebb and flow of the *ecclesiastical year* give him a wide variety of emotional life:
      a) **Advent:** With its recalling of man's fall and the subsequent winter of the Old Law; the undying hope of the Jewish people listening to prophets and king who foretold and foreshadowed the coming Messias.
      b) **Christmas and Epiphany:** With the coming of the God-man to earth, and the consequent joy of humanity.
      c) **The Sundays after Epiphany:** With the hidden life of the Savior at Nazareth as a model for the relatively obscure life of the average man.

d) **Lent:** With its sorrow for sin, its gratitude to Christ who died for our sins and saved us from their consequences.

e) **Easter:** With its realization of the victory of the Risen Christ, the glory that lies ahead, and the certainty of our own resurrection from death.

f) **Ascension:** With its glimpse of heaven and the consequent increase of our hope.

g) **Pentecost:** With the coming of the Holy Ghost, the birth of the Church, and the strength and comfort and guidance He brought to mankind.

h) **The Feasts of the year:** Each recalling:

    (1) Some event in the *life of Christ.*

    (2) Some mystery in the *life of His mother.*

    (3) The heroic *lives of Apostles* who preached the message of Christ to the world; of the *martyrs* who died for truth; of the *confessors* who lived and taught truth; of the *virgins* whose lives were examples of shining sinlessness.

V. **The Chief Devotions of the Church are:**

  A. *To God the Father:*

    1. All Masses are offered to Him.

    2. The "Our Father" is the Church's favorite prayer.

    3. He is honored in all prayers, all services, all ritual, as the Creator, the Father of all.

  B. *To God the Son:*

    1. He is our Victim and High Priest in the Mass.

    2. All Eucharistic devotion tends to Him.

    3. He is man's elder brother, leader, and captain.

    4. He is reverenced as the eternal Judge.

    5. Hence:

      a) *Benediction,* the worship of the Blessed Sacrament, is all directly His.

      b) *Special devotions* of universal appeal are directed to Him: e.g.,

        (1) The devotion to the *Sacred Heart,* symbol of Christ's boundless love of mankind.

        (2) The devotion to the *Passion* of the Savior, which wrought the salvation of the world.

      c) Special devotions suited to special types of men and women: e.g., to

(1) The Infant Savior.

(2) The Boy Jesus.

(3) The Bridegroom of souls.

(4) The comforter and consoler.

(5) Christ, as physician, lawyer, carpenter, scholar, etc.

(6) The risen and triumphant Conqueror of sin and death.

C. The Holy Ghost:

1. **Devotion to the Holy Ghost** began on the day which is sometimes called "The Birthday of the Church," Pentecost Sunday.

a) *The Holy Ghost then came upon the Apostles,* filling their souls with courage and their minds with wisdom that changed them from cowards into world conquerors.

b) The Apostles gave the Holy Ghost to others through the imposition of Hands in the *Sacrament of Confirmation.*

c) Today the Bishop gives to the faithful this same indwelling of the Holy Ghost in Confirmation, so that the Third Person of the Blessed Trinity:

(1) Chooses the body and souls of *the faithful as His temple.*

(2) Is present as *the source of grace,* Himself Uncreated Grace.

(3) Is the fountain of *special sevenfold gifts* and helps, enlightening the mind, strengthening the will, giving comfort and peace and joy.

Note: It is the indwelling of the Holy Spirit that gives *to the Church:*

1. Its infallibility in teaching.

2. Its strength against persecution.

It is the indwelling of the Holy Spirit that gives *to the individual:*

1. Wisdom that is divine.

2. Strength and courage in time of adversity.

2. Hence, Catholic devotion:

a) Causes many colleges to begin their year with the *Mass of the Holy Ghost* or special prayers to the Holy Ghost. This brings down upon the students special help and guidance in their studies, and special strength against temptation.

b) Inspires Catholics to turn to the God dwelling in their hearts:

(1) *For wisdom and knowledge,* both divine and human, i.e., knowledge of God and supernatural things and knowledge and success in their studies.

(2) *For courage* in the face of the world's difficulties and persecutions.

(3) *For strength* in time of temptation.

c) Sets aside *Pentecost and its Octave* as among the most solemn feasts of the year, with very special privileges and indulgences that can be gained by the faithful at this time.

D. *To Mary:*

1. Who is mother of God and humanity, since she is mother of the God-man, Jesus Christ and was given as the mother of Christ to us who are His younger brothers and saints: "Son, behold thy mother."

2. **Devotion to Mary** consists in:

a) *Imitation of her* by her loyal sons and daughters. She of all mankind served Christ best. She was the perfect example of what a mere human being could be.

b) *Honoring her through:*

(1) The dignified and beautiful celebration of her many *feasts and the months, May and October,* dedicated to her.

(2) Careful tending of her *altars and shrines.* These are public or private according to devotion.

(3) *Prayers* that express her praise and call for her protectection: e.g.,

(a) **The Rosary,** which is:

i) *Vocal prayer;* the salute of faithful subjects to their Queen, using the salute of an angel, the salute of the great St. Elizabeth, and the salute of the grateful Church.

ii) *Mental prayer;* the thoughtful consideration of the mysteries of her joyful, sorrowful, and glorious life.

(b) Prayers such as the **Angelus,** the **Memorare,** the **Little Office,** the **Litany.**

E. *To the saints:*

1. A knowledge of their life inspires brave souls to imitation. There are saints who have:

a) *A universal appeal.*

(1) *St. Joseph,* foster father of Christ, patron of the uni-

versal Church, and guardian of all ages and classes of mankind.

(2) *The Apostles,* who were the foundation stones of the Church.

(3) *The Doctors of the Church,* who taught and explained the message of Christ: St. Jerome; St. Augustine; St. Thomas; St. Francis de Sales.

(4) The great *Missionaries,* who appeal to all heroic souls: St. Patrick; St. Francis Xavier.

(5) Saints of a *special Christlike quality:* St. Francis of Assisi; St. Theresa, the Little Flower.

b) The special *national patron saints:*

(1) St. Patrick for Ireland.

(2) St. George for England.

(3) St. Denis and St. Joan of Arc for France.

(4) St. Boniface for Germany.

c) Saints who appeal to *special groups or classes:*

(1) *Namesakes,* for whom Catholics are called in Baptism.

(2) Saints of *particular times of life:*

(a) *Childhood* — St. Hugh of Lincoln, St. Agnes, St. Pancratius, St. Philomene.

(b) *Youth* — St. Aloysius, St. Gabriel of the Passion, St. Cecilia, St. Agatha, St. Tarcisius, St. Dorothy.

(c) *Married Life* — St. Louis of France, St. Frances of Rome.

(3) Saints of *particular professions;* each profession has its patron saint, e.g.:

(a) Doctors — St. Cosmas and Damien.

(b) Lawyers — St. Ives.

(c) Artists — St. Luke.

(d) Soldiers — St. Sebastian.

(4) Saints of *particular devotions:*

(a) St. Jude — hopeless cases.

(b) St. Blase — throat diseases.

(c) St. Roch — illness.

(d) St. Christopher — travelers.

(e) St. Anne — Happy marriages.

(f) Our Lady of Loretto and the Archangels — Aviation.

F. To *the Angels:*

1. God's messengers to whom is intrusted the care of mankind.

a) Read the story of Tobias:

"He hath given his angels charge over thee."

Christ and the consoling angel in His agony in Gethsemane.

2. Who are specially assigned to each Christian as Angel Guardians.

a) "Their angels see the face of your father who is in heaven," was what Christ said of the little children of Judea.

VI. **Hence, Catholic Devotion is:**

A. As *varied* as the varieties of human temperament.

B. Always *grounded in sound logic,* proven truths, and reason.

C. *Suited to human needs,* instincts, and emotional inclinations.

D. Giving men a *keener appreciation* of their supernatural destiny.

E. *Uniting them more closely to God* and His saints.

F. Allowing man's intellectual convictions *an external manifestation* and thus reënforcing and strengthening them. Man's loyalty of will is given an exterior and emotional release.

Problems and Discussions

1. A non-Catholic says that he thinks "devotions" are weak and effeminate and unnecessary. Show him that there is a natural devotion by which all men tend to express externally their deep internal convictions and emotions.

2. If man is a creature composed of body and soul, must he have an emotional expression of his religion? Illustrate your answer.

3. Discuss this statement: One of the most beautiful words in our language is the word *devoted.*

4. Show how the cross of Christ corresponds to the flag of a nation. What external honor would necessarily be due to the cross?

5. The highest compliment paid to a leader is this: "He has won the loyalty and devotion of his men." Why is this true of Christ? How can this loyalty and devotion be shown to Him?

6. Discuss this statement: "Non-Catholic faith and worship is emotionally and artistically satisfactory."

7. Analyze this statement: The saints are the heroes and heroines of the Church and deserve at least the same honors as are paid by a nation to its distinguished great. Is this done in the Church? Is it done in non-Catholic groups?

8. Why is there need in the Church for a variety of devotions?

9. List some devotions not mentioned in the main discussion and indicate for what sort of people they are appropriate.

10. Is the Church wise to make the Mass beautiful in its music, vestments, incense, lights, whole ritual?
11. What effect upon a man's religious life could be gained through an exact following of the ecclesiastical year?
12. What are the main feasts of and devotions to Christ; Mary?
13. Discuss the statement: The rosary can be used by the most simple and the most learned people.
14. List some of the following types of saints, besides those mentioned in the main discussion:
    a) Patrons of various nations.
    b) Patrons of professions.
    c) Patrons of particular ages of men and women.
    d) Favorite namesake saints.
15. Would you call a son or daughter by a name that was not borne by some saint? Why or why not?
16. Indicate to a non-Catholic the deep human wisdom and the divine fitness of the Church's attitude toward devotions.

Suggested Readings

PAMPHLETS

America Press:
The Liturgical Movement, Ellard, S.J.
The Paulist Press:
Devotion to the Holy Spirit, McSarley, C.S.P.
Lent and Its Meaning and Purpose, Gueranger.
The Catholic Truth Society:
The Sacraments, Martindale, S.J.
Catholic Practices, Hornyold.

BOOKS

Bouchard, *Chief Catholic Doctrines* (Kenedy).
See the *Catholic Encyclopedia:* "Devotion"; "The Sacraments"; "Grace"; "The Holy Ghost"; *et passim.*

Chapter XVIII

AN OUTLINE OF CATHOLIC DOCTRINE

I. **The teachings of the Catholic Church,** which are simply the teachings of Jesus Christ as the inevitable conclusion and fulfillment of the original teachings of the Old Law are:

  A. *A logical and reasonable unit.*

  B. *Wonderfully beautiful and satisfying.*

  C. *Proved:*

  1. By their *appeal to reason* and their conformity with man's desires.

  2. From the *divine authority* of Christ and His appointed teachers, the Apostles.

  3. From the *explanations of His infallible teacher,* the Church.

Here, we make no effort to prove these teachings. They are proved throughout the religion and philosophy course. They are in this discussion presented as a connected series of truths forming together a reasonable explanation of the relation between God and men and of the way by which a man serves his Creator and wins the happiness for which he was destined. (This chapter is to be taken as an amplification of Chapter XVI).

II. **The Series of Catholic Truths:**

  A. **There is a God,** personal and infinitely knowing and powerful.

  1. This is proved:

    a) By arguments from reason.

    b) By His own revelations of Himself.

      (1) He is a person, because He has an intellect that plans and a will that carries out that plan.

      (2) He is infinite, because He must contain without dependence and in completeness the perfections which He imparts to the universe.

  B. **God created mankind** as a part of the tremendous universe. (This was discussed in Chapter XVII.)

  C. **God has promised eternal happiness** in the company of Himself to the men who live well.

116

    1. Man's immortality is proved:

      a) By his desire for perfect happiness.

      b) By the clear revelation of God and Christ, His divine Son.

D. And He has *threatened with an eternal loss* of this happiness and of Himself those men who live badly.

    1. A man by living badly rejects God from his life. This voluntary rejection of God becomes eternal through death. A man who lives evilly throws away his chance of improving the world. His evil conduct makes him a criminal unworthy of a reward. But as man is immortal, immortality without happiness is inevitable.

    2. This idea of reward or punishment has been held by all nations, pagan, Jewish, or Christian.

E. **But man:**

    1. Who had been:

      a) *Adopted as the son of God,* and His heir.

      b) *Endowed with grace,* implying the power ultimately to see God face to face and to possess Him in eternal happiness.

      c) *Given a mastery over his passions.*

    2. *Rebelled against God;* threw away his right to be God's son and heir.

      a) *Lost grace* and the right to eternal happiness.

      b) *Lost the complete mastery* over his passions.

      c) This was the **original sin:**

        (1) *A personal sin* of Adam's.

        (2) *The consequences of which* were passed on to Adam's sons and daughters, as his rights and privileges would have been passed had he been faithful. His sons and daughters were born:

          (*a*) Without the right to divine adoption.

          (*b*) Without their inheritance, heaven.

          (*c*) With will and intellect weakened and inclined toward sin. Thus we inherited our father's sin.

    3. *God,* however, *promised to send a Redeemer* who would:

      a) *Take the punishment* due for this crime.

      b) *Satisfy the injured Father* and the insulted King.

      c) *Regain for men God's sonship,* grace, and their right to eternal happiness.

F. **God revealed Himself,** His commandments, His desire for love, the method by which He wishes to be honored and served:

1. *To His Patriarchs, Prophets, and Kings of the Old Law.*
   a) This was recorded in a series of historical books, whose writing was inspired by God, called the Old Testament.
2. *Through His Son, Our Lord, Jesus Christ,* who taught:
   a) The will of His Father.
   b) The way in which to worship Him correctly.
   c) The means of winning everlasting life.
      (1) These means are set forth:
         (*a*) In the historical and inspired books of the *Gospels.*
         (*b*) In the equally inspired books of the *Acts of the Apostles* and of the *Epistles.*
      (2) These means were *intrusted to His Apostles:*
         (*a*) Who were the foundation stones of an *infallible Church.*
         (*b*) The men to whom He gave power:
            i) *To teach truth* without the possibility of error.
            ii) *To lead men safely* and surely to their eternal destiny.
            iii) *To supply them with all the helps* they needed, especially through the sacraments.
      (3) They are further set forth:
         (*a*) In the teaching of the *Popes and Councils.*
         (*b*) In the teaching of the *Fathers of the Church* and of her ecclesiastical and ascetical writers.
         (*c*) In the pious conscience of the *devout faithful.*
3. **This Jesus Christ** who came to teach men God's will and to establish a Church was:
   a) *The Son of God* (the Second Person of the Blessed Trinity):
      (1) Who claimed to be divine.
      (2) Who acted as divine.
      (3) Who proved Himself to be divine.
4. Because He was divine, His actions were great enough to satisfy God the Father.
5. Because He was man, He could act as a member of the human race which by sins (those of Adam and his descendants) had offended and wronged God.
6. *So He offered His life on the cross:*
   a) Dying as a criminal *to satisfy for the crimes* of men.
   b) Offering just punishment to satisfy *a just and offended God.*

c) Making again available for man by this act:
    (1) The *lost favor* with His Father.
    (2) *Sanctifying grace* by means of which man becomes possessed of the right to eternal happiness.
7. Hence, Christ's death on the cross:
    a) Wiped out Adam's guilt.
    b) Restored to man, if he wished to lay hold on them, the most precious of the things Adam had cast away.
    c) Reopened heaven to mankind, provided man accepts this freely and deliberately.

G. Christ made it possible that all mankind might be incorporated in Him. He made possible the **Mystical Body** so that:
1. Men could *share in the effects* of His death and resurrection.
2. Men could be regarded by God the Father as *united with Christ,* His beloved Son, co-heirs, brothers of Jesus Christ.
3. Men could receive directly from Christ by reason of *this union, effected by sanctifying grace,* the power in the after-life:
    a) *Of seeing God face to face* in heaven.
    b) *Of possessing God* in endless happiness.

H. Man, however, must do this willingly. God will not force him to:
1. *Accept grace* and its consequences, which Adam threw away.
2. *Unite himself with Christ,* so that God the Father will love and accept him as His son.
3. Man does all this through the exercise of *the acts of the virtues,* chiefest among which are:
    a) *Faith;* i.e., the divine virtue by which we firmly believe the truths which God has revealed.
    b) *Hope;* i.e., the divine virtue by which we firmly trust that God will give us eternal life and the means of obtaining it.
    c) *Charity;* i.e., the divine virtue by which we love God above all things for His own sake, and our neighbor as ourselves for the love of God.

I. To make this possible and, in a measure, **easier:**
1. Christ instituted His Sacraments which are fountains of grace, both sanctifying and actual. Thus grace puts us again in possession of the essentially necessary things, once lost through Adam, now regained through Christ.
    a) *Baptism:* a sacrament which cleanses us from original sin, makes us Christians, children of God, and heirs of heaven.

    b) Confirmation: a sacrament through which we receive the Holy Ghost to make us strong and perfect Christians and soldiers of Jesus Christ.

    c) Holy Eucharist: a sacrament which gives to the soul the living presence of Jesus Christ, increases sanctifying grace and all virtues in the soul, unites us to Himself, and nourishes our soul with His divine life.

    d) Penance: a sacrament in which the sins committed after baptism are forgiven.

    e) Extreme Unction: a sacrament which increases sanctifying grace in the soul and gives man the strength to retain it in His final struggle with temptation, while preparing him for eternity.

    f) Holy Orders: a sacrament which provides a constant supply of priests who can carry on the work of Christ and the giving of grace.

    g) Matrimony: a sacrament which blesses and gives strength to a man and woman who mean to bring into the world sons of God and heirs of heaven.

J. **Christ instituted the Mass:**

  1. So that men could continuously feel *the effects of His reparation* to God the Father for sin.

  2. So that God the Father could continuously *see mankind offering Him* its best and finest Member, Jesus Christ.

  3. So that the grace and powers won by the *death of Christ* would always be easily *accessible to mankind.*

  4. **The Mass** is thus the unbloody and painless repetition of the sacrifice of the cross; and it is:

    a) The central act of Catholic worship.

    b) The source of grace and power.

    c) Which men can offer to God the Father and to which they can unite themselves, offering themselves with Christ the Victim. Christ with men offers the Mass: men together with Christ are offered.

K. **The acts by which man loses his sonship** and title to heaven, by which he spoils God's work and harms his fellow men are forbidden in:

  1. *The Ten Commandments.*

L. **The acts by which man proves his devotion** to his Father, his right to eternal happiness, and by which he advances God's work and helps and improves his fellow men are called, *The Virtues,* and are contained chiefly in the commands, counsels, and beatitudes of Christ, the commandments of the Church.

M. **To strengthen men in this important struggle,** to comfort them in time of trial, Christ sent the **Third Person of the Blessed Trinity,** the Holy Ghost:

1. On *Pentecost,* to the Apostles.

2. In the Sacrament of *Confirmation,* to all those who receive it.

3. **The Holy Ghost:**

   a) Dwells in the soul of the baptized as in His temple.

   b) Is an immediate and present *source of strength,* grace, power.

   c) Helps the soul in its struggle against temptation.

   d) Is the source of *divine wisdom.*

   e) Brings special virtues, such as peace, joy, gentleness, patience, courage, wisdom, and filial fear of the Lord.

N. **Hence, God, while one in nature, contains three Persons:**

1. God the *Father:* the Creator.

2. God the *Son:* the Redeemer.

3. God the *Holy Ghost:* the Sanctifier.

4. This we know:

   a) From the clear teachings of Christ.

   b) From the action of the three divine Persons, manifesting themselves.

5. This is a mystery; but it is not strange that the limited mind of man should fail to comprehend the infinite nature of God.

O. **God chose out of all the world one woman to be His mother.**

1. His angel visited her, saluted her with high praise and asked her to be the mother of the Savior.

2. The Holy Spirit was her Spouse. The Holy Ghost formed the infant Christ in her womb without any human father.

3. She was the tabernacle of the God-man for nine months; His guardian and protector during childhood; His sympathetic companion through young manhood; His comfort on Calvary.

4. Hence:

   a) As His mother, she has power to influence Him and to obtain favors from Him.

   b) As one of our race, she loves us and intercedes for us, whom she regards as her children.

P. **God the Savior, so that these essential truths** would safely and constantly be taught to mankind, instituted:

1. **His Infallible Church.** (See Chapters XIII and XIV.)

Q. *At the head of this Church He placed St. Peter* and his successors:

1. With infallibility. The gates of hell should not prevail against him.
2. With universal jurisdiction over all the faithful. "Feed My lambs; feed My sheep."
3. With the "power of the keys," that is, authority to bind and loose in the name of Christ. "I will give you the keys of the Kingdom of Heaven."
4. And made him the center of unity so that there would be "one flock and one shepherd."

Problems and Discussions

1. An unbeliever says: "The Catholic Faith is a silly and disconnected muddle of unrelated and undignified fables." Have you an answer?
2. Do any of these dogmas (as is constantly said by those who do not understand them) seem stupid or hampering or undignified?
3. It has been said that one of the strongest proofs for the truth of the Catholic Faith is its logical connection and remarkable harmony and unity. Discuss this.
4. Do you see any similarity between the children of a father who squandered a large inheritance and the human race as the sons of Adam?
5. If an eternal reward is promised for well-doing, why is an eternal punishment or loss of that reward inevitable for a man who throws away his sonship of God, his claim to heaven, and the divine powers and grace given him?
6. What are the main ways in which God has revealed Himself to mankind?
7. Speaking of the mystery of the Blessed Trinity, wise men have sometimes said: "If my limited mind could really understand God, I should know that He is not really God." Analyze this statement.
8. The crucifixion has been called the pivotal moment in history. Why?
9. Discuss this statement: Only a God-man could make reparation for the crimes of man against God.
10. What place has the Catholic Church in this whole scheme of Christ's teachings?
11. What is the relative importance of Christ's life and Christ's death for mankind?

12. Was it wise of Christ by establishing the Mass to continue in a pain-less and unbloody manner the effects of His death?
13. What are some of the effects upon a man of his union with Jesus Christ?
14. Why did Christ leave men free to accept His redemption and this restoration of the powers and sonship lost by Adam?
15. Show the relation of the sacraments to the restoration of man's lost powers and privileges.
16. What is the place of the Holy Ghost in the Catholic doctrine and God's scheme for the world?
17. Discuss the statement: "Mary is unnecessary to Christian religion."
18. A non-Catholic argues: "The Ten Commandments are a ball and chain around the ankle of a free man." Answer him.

Suggested Readings

PAMPHLETS

The Paulist Press:
   The Catholic Faith, Harney, C.S.P.
   What the Catholic Church Is and What She Teaches, Hull, S.J.
   Personal Immortality, Downey.
   The Mystical Body of Christ, Bellanti, S.J.
The Catholic Truth Society:
   The Supernatural Life, Vassall-Phillips.
   Words of Life, Martindale, S.J.
   Catholic Doctrines, Hornyold.
America Press:
   What Then Must I Believe? Lonergan.

BOOKS

Knox, *Belief of Catholics* (Harpers).
Martindale, *Sacramental System* (Macmillan).
Martindale, *The Faith of the Roman Church* (Richard G. Smith).

Chapter XIX

AN OUTLINE OF SCHOLASTIC PHILOSOPHY

I. As a general rule, **Catholic colleges** pride themselves on their courses of Philosophy. They offer them:

    A. As giving the student *a reasonable, clear, unified, and inspiring attitude* toward life.

    B. As giving him a dignified and rational standard for action and conduct.

    C. As establishing him *in correct relationship* to the world, his fellow men, and all the elements that surround his life.

    D. As helping to establish the *fundamentals on which religion and faith* securely and firmly rest.

From the beginning, apologists for Christianity stressed the importance of a firm, rational foundation for faith. The Church from the beginning was deeply interested in philosophy and realized that it was possible to prove from reason the existence of God, the fact of a human soul and its qualities, the general laws governing thought and the pursuit of truth. Hence:

    1. The first **Christian Apologists** showed the Roman Emperors how Christianity agreed in its love of truth with the best pagan philosophers.

    2. The **Fathers of the Church** regarded philosophy as sharing with theology the supreme claim to man's interest.

    3. **Pagan philosophers** were widely studied and their best thought used in Christianity.

II. **Scholastic Philosophy,** the philosophy taught today in Catholic colleges, is a magnificent, orderly, and unified *synthesis* of:

    A. *The best thought* of the greatest of *pagan thinkers,* Aristotle.

    B. The profound study of the *Christian philosophers of the Middle Ages:* Albert the Great, Thomas of Aquin, Bonaventure, Duns Scotus, Abelard, and the other brilliant Schoolmen.

    C. The developed thought of the *philosophers of Renaissance* and *post-Renaissance days.*

III. In modern times this system has been subjected to serious study and revision *to meet the development of modern science* and the extension of modern discovery. These **Neo-Scholastics or New Schoolmen** received a great impetus from the encouragement of Leo XIII. Notable among them is the famous Cardinal Mercier.

Note 1: This outline is very brief. The Philosophy Department of the college develops, explains, and proves the truths of Scholastic Philosophy here indicated.

Note 2: Only the barest skeleton of these truths and the content of the system is indicated.

IV. **Scholastic Philosophy** *is too little known* outside of the Catholic Church. This is due to a number of factors:

    A. *It is Catholic in origin,* and hence was dropped by most Protestants following the Reformation.

    B. It experienced, as great schools of thought do, *a period of decline,* during which progressive thinkers felt it was occupied with unimportant questions. They forgot its great fundamental theses and left it for new lines of thought.

    C. Since opponents of the Church *incorrectly* stated that Scholastic Philosophy was *only another form of Theology,* many philosophers did not bother to investigate it.

    D. Its greatest textbooks are *written in Latin,* a language which many philosophers today cannot read.

    E. *Since the Reformation,* philosophy has undergone so many changes and such shifts of viewpoints that:

        1. Many systems are mutually *contradictory.*

        2. *Almost every* sort of answer is given to the most fundamental question of life and existence and a Supreme Being and truth and right.

        3. Many are *fundamentally skeptical* of the possibility of attaining truth.

    F. Hence **many modern philosophers;**

        1. Regard philosophy *as the history of human opinions* rather than as a unified system of thought explaining realities.

        2. Regard the *discovery of truth as less interesting* than the study of human thinking.

        3. Have *lost belief in the possibility of finding ultimate truth,* since the various systems of philosophy so thoroughly contradict one another.

4. However, a great awakening of interest has manifested it-self during the past ten years. Many non-Catholic universi-ties, notably, Harvard, Chicago, Pennsylvania, now give reg-ular courses in Scholastic Philosophy. T. S. Eliot has called Jacques Maritain (Scholastic Philosopher of the present) the greatest living philosopher in Europe. St. Thomas is being widely read by the non-Catholic world, notably in France.

V. Among the **opponents** of Scholastic Philosophy it is important to remember that:

A. There is much *serious love of truth* and much brave and splen-did effort to discover it.

B. Each system of thought has *elements of truth* in it, some more, some less.

C. There is, however, as *much discord* among philosophies out-side of Scholastic Philosophy as there is among non-Catholic creeds and churches.

D. The quest for truth in some popular philosophies begins with the *presupposition that truth cannot be discovered.*

VI. **Philosophy** is the study of truth by the light of reason.

A. *It investigates the final reason* why things exist and explains their first origins, their relation to one another, and their ulti-mate purpose.

B. *It studies man, the universe,* all visible and invisible beings to find out what they are in themselves and what relation they bear to one another.

C. *It explains the great questions* that man is always asking:

1. Whence came the world?
2. Why does the world exist?
3. What is truth?
4. Is there a Supreme Being and of what nature?
5. What meaning has life?
6. Is there a life after this life?
7. How must a man act?

Note: Philosophy is sometimes called "the handmaid of theology." This does not mean that it is subordinated to theology or really a part of it.

1. Philosophy studies truth by the light of reason. Theology largely studies truth that has been revealed by God.

2. However, a thing cannot be true in theology and false in philosophy,

as a thing cannot be true in chemistry and false in physics. Hence, some revealed truths of theology are the same as truths discovered by philosophy.

3. The truths of philosophy lay a reasonable groundwork on which theology can build. Thus philosophy proves God, the existence and immortality of the soul, the credibility of history. On these truths theology builds.

VII. **Scholastic Philosophy**, unlike many philosophies of the day, is not negative, pessimistic, or destructive; it is *positive, affirmative, constructive, and destructive only of error.*
Thus:
   A. *Skepticism* denies all possibility of discovering truth.
   B. *Atheism* denies a Supreme Being.
   C. *Kantianism* implicitly denies all possibility of knowing things with certainty.
   D. *Materialism* denies anything except what can be seen, touched, measured.
   E. *Determinism* denies freedom to a man to choose his course of action.

VIII. **Scholastic Philosophy** is consistently affirmatory and positive:
   A. It is *proved* by the most convincing and solid arguments.
      1. From reason.
      2. From investigation of scientific data.
      3. From the fitness of the truth to human dignity and aspiration.
   B. *A man can live by this philosophy.* Many others he has to deny practically in order to live effectively.
For example: If a man argues that he has no free will, he can only live by acting as if he had a free will. If he argues that he cannot know truth, he at least holds the truth that he cannot know truth, and constantly accepts truth from newspapers, friends, science, history, etc.
   C. *It is in line with man's aspirations* and is borne out by his experience.

IX. In briefest outline, the **course of Scholastic Philosophy** runs thus (sometimes a different order is used in philosophy departments):
   A. Before the student begins the search for truth:
      1. He *studies the rules* by which the mind must be guided if it is to discover truth.

a) The laws of reasoning.

b) The methods of induction and deduction.

c) How to build and recognize a true argument.

d) The scientific approach to truth.

2. *He learns how to detect:*

a) A false statement.

b) A faulty argument.

c) An incorrect deduction or induction.

3. This is the study of the "tools of truth."

B. He then discovers:

1. That under certain circumstances there is such a thing as *truth.*

2. *What truth is* in itself and what different kinds of truth there are.

3. *The sources* from which truth can be sought and found.

C. He then determines how far and under what circumstances *a man is capable of learning truth.*

1. He finds that under certain circumstances his *senses* report correctly the objects of the material world.

2. He finds that under certain circumstances his *intellect* attains truth, and his reasoning faculty draws new truths from old ones.

D. He checks carefully the conditions under which the *other sources* of knowledge bring truth:

1. The *testimony* of fellow men.

2. The trustworthiness of *history* in its primary and secondary sources.

E. Then in *a most important branch* of philosophy (that can only be in briefest form indicated here):

1. He finds that *all things* have certain elements in common and certain things in which they differ.

2. He studies the *elements common to all:* Existence, possibility, unity, truth, beauty.

3. He studies the *elements in which they differ:* Dependence or independence, perfection or imperfection, completeness or incompleteness.

4. He studies *essential relationships* like: Cause and effect, purpose or end.

F. About him is a *visible universe.*

1. He finds that it does not necessarily exist and that it could

not have caused its own existence but must owe its existence to *some power outside itself.*

2. He examines *its material* to find out what ultimately makes one thing different from another and precisely that which it is.

3. He studies the *ultimate constituent elements* of nature, using the information given him by physics and chemistry, but going beyond them to the final elements of matter.

G. He studies the *living world* and finds:

1. That *life is essentially different from nonlife,* because it nourishes itself from within, repairs from within all waste, grows from within, and reproduces its own kind.

2. He studies *animals* and finds them *essentially different from plants* because of sensation.

H. He then studies *man himself:*

1. He finds that man is *essentially different from animals,* because he thinks, wills, plans, applies consciously means to an end, speaks, aspires to things beyond the earth.

2. Though his body is made of chemical elements like those of the rest of material creation, man has *within him something different* that shows itself:

   a) *In mental and intellectual processes* that cannot be produced by chemistry or physics; for this "something different" thinks of spiritual things, of abstract things, and reasons.

   b) *In processes of a free will,* by which it chooses freely one thing in preference to another. He knows all purely material things are bound by the laws of chemistry and physics and cannot choose. Therefore man has something which is not material and which makes it possible for him to choose.

   c) This "something different" he calls the **Soul,** and finds out that it is:

   (1) *Simple,* not made up of parts.

   (2) *Spiritual,* not essentially depending upon the brain which it uses as an instrument.

   (3) *Immortal,* destined for a life beyond this immediate and present one.

I. From a close *study of the world,* its plan, order, law, motion, lack of necessary existence, immensity, he proves the existence of a **Supreme Being:**

1. Who must contain *all perfections,* otherwise He could not have given to the world its immense perfections.
2. Who is a *person* because:
   a) He has *intelligence;* as is proved from the plan He put into the world.
   b) Who has a *will,* because the world is ruled by law, and laws demand the will of a lawgiver.
3. This Being has among His *qualities:*
   a) Beauty: Because the world is full of beauty which He gave it.
   b) Power: Because only supreme power could have produced this world.
   c) Immensity: Because the universe is vast.
   d) Providence: Because the world and every creature in it is magnificently ordered and cared for.
   e) Independence: Because all else is dependent and demands this independent and self-existing being upon whom it can depend.

J. Finally the student studies his *relationships with all other beings,* and finds that he is:

1. *A social being,* destined by nature for association with his fellows.
2. *A religious being,* with certain obligations to God.
3. *A moral being,* with justice to fulfill and laws to obey.
4. *A being with rights* that he may justly claim from others.

K. Finally *he learns to apply* and actually does apply what he has learned *to the practical problems of life.*

Note 1: In the Catholic Church and in the Catholic Church alone does all this magnificent reasoning process precede and underlie the systematic study of religious dogma. Hence, it may be said that the Catholic Church is the one reasonable and logical religion in the world.

Note 2: With most of this philosophy the believing Protestant will readily agree. Unfortunately, ignorance of Catholic philosophy keeps many sincere Protestants from using its power against a doubting world.

Note 3: The average clear thinker would find this logical, reasonable, and intellectually satisfactory. However, in many cases he never actually comes in contact with this system of reasonable thought.

X. Thus the **Catholic student:**

    A. *Proves from reason the existence of God* before he studies God's revelation of Himself through religion.

    B. *Proves the existence of a soul* from reason before he proves it from the teachings of Christ and the Bible.

    C. *Proves that the New Testament is correct history* and that history can be believed before he studies what Christ did and taught in that history.

    D. *Proves that man is bound by law* before he studies the law that nature and God impose upon Him.

Note: Scholastic Philosophy is not a complete, finished, compact group of truths eliminating further study, investigation, or development. It is constantly being explored and developed. Truths are constantly being re-investigated. Each new fact of science is considered in its effects upon this philosophy. It is alive, alert, modifying itself and developing under the guidance of keen minds and of advancing science and discovery.

Problems and Discussions

1. If Scholastic Philosophy is so important and sane and valuable, why is it important for a Catholic student to receive his full college education in a Catholic college?

2. Indicate to a Protestant that Scholastic Philosophy would help him to defend the reasonableness of his life and his fundamental beliefs.

3. Why cannot a truth that is true in theology be false in philosophy? Illustrate by comparisons from other fields.

4. Name some notable modern Catholic philosophers.

5. A non-Catholic student in a state university says to you: "I don't see how Scholastic Philosophy can be so important. It was mentioned only in passing in my philosophy course." Answer his difficulty.

6. If the non-Catholic philosophies are as discordant and contradictory as the non-Catholic churches and creeds, what does this seem to indicate?

7. Discuss from the standpoint of common sense and your own reasoning processes some of the following statements taught by popular philosophies:

    a) *Pantheism:* Everything in the world is a part of God.

    b) *Pantheism:* Happiness consists in losing one's identity by absorption in the divine all-spirit.

    c) *Materialism:* Man is only an improved animal.

    d) *Materialism:* The desire and idea of immortality is simply a terrible illusion.

    e) *Idealistic Monism:* There is no such thing as matter. Everything is spirit and a manifestation of the divine mind.

    f) Materialism: This is an unplanned and lawless world.

    g) Materialism (another group): This world is bound by universal law, but a law that requires no lawgiver.

    h) Amoralism: Man finds in his nature no law.

    i) Skeptics: We can be certain of nothing.

    j) Historical skeptics: Under all circumstances, history brings only probability.

    k) Hedonism: The highest purpose of life is pleasure.

8. Discuss in its effects upon human conduct the following statements of popular philosophies:

    a) Man has no free will and cannot choose between right and wrong.

    b) Man is not essentially different from the beasts.

    c) Fate decrees our destiny no matter how we may try to shape it.

    d) The principle of the Survival of the Fittest must be applied to the relationships of man with man and nation with nation.

    e) The quest for truth is futile and an illusion.

    f) There is no life beyond the grave.

    g) Morality and the laws governing sex are merely customs that change with various generations.

    h) Man is not a social animal.

9. Why can it be said of Catholic Philosophy that it treats the whole of life and treats it in accord with man's dignity?

10. A non-Catholic says: "The Catholic Church asks a man to lay aside his reason." Can you answer him?

11. Why is Catholic Philosophy especially needed today?

Suggested Readings

PAMPHLETS

    The Queen's Work Press:
      You Can't Live That Way, Lord, S.J.
    Paulist Press:
      Philosophy and Belief, Pace.
    The Catholic Truth Society:
      The Powers and Origin of the Soul, Northcote.

BOOKS

    Lord, *Armchair Philosophy* (America Press).
    McNabb, *Catholic Church and Philosophy* (Calvert Series) (Macmillan).
    Ward, *The Catholic Church and the Appeal to Reason* (Macmillan).
    Ferrier, *The Revival of Scholastic Philosophy* (Columbia Press).
    See the *Catholic Encyclopedia:* "Philosophy"; "Scholasticism"; *et passim.*

Chapter XX

LOYALTY TO THE PERSON OF JESUS CHRIST

I. **Success in Life** is bound up largely with **loyalty to persons:**

    A. A man succeeds often largely because of *the inspiration of his mother or his wife* or the love of his children.

    B. Men follow *professions* or careers or take up sports because of their *admiration for other men* who have succeeded in these lines.

      1. Great doctors inspire other doctors.

      2. Great lawyers gather to them young aspirants.

      3. Young men and women follow the example of noted sportsmen, authors, business men, actors, artists.

    C. *A nation builds its traditions* almost less upon its institutions and forms of external government than *upon the great men* who promoted or embodied those principles:

      1. George Washington stands for the spirit of the Revolution:

      2. Robert E. Lee is the spirit of the chivalrous South.

      3. Thomas Jefferson is the inspiration of the Democratic Party.

      4. Lincoln is the ideal of typical American manhood.

      5. Mussolini is the incarnation of modern Italy.

      6. Lenin and Stalin are the concrete figures that embody the ideals of the Soviet.

      7. Darwin is the human symbol for the theory of Evolution.

      8. Edison is the inspiration and ideal of modern invention.

II. The Catholic who is intelligently and really aware of the meaning of his faith:

    A. Knows that his *religion* will be:

      1. *Enthusiastic* instead of dull and uninteresting.

      2. *Spontaneous* instead of forced.

      3. *Inspired* instead of endured.

    B. If he realizes that the *Catholic religion:*

      1. Was given to mankind by *the world's most inspiring figure.*

      2. Was established by the *One who lived and died* for the sake of mankind.

      3. Contains *essentially the truths and laws* which He gave to men.

III. **The intelligent Catholic** follows and gives his religious loyalty to the person of the world's Savior, Jesus Christ, our Lord.

Note: In a later treatise, the divinity of Jesus Christ will be proved, His historical character studied, and the message and mission He exercised as Messias explained. Here we consider Him merely as a Leader who inspires the utmost loyalty and love.

IV. **Christ** is the **Central Figure** in all history.
    A. The *Old Testament kings and prophets* prepared for Him, pre-figured Him, foretold Him:
        1. *Adam,* the father of the human race; Christ, who undid the evil of Adam's fall.
        2. *Abraham,* the father of the chosen people; Christ, the Father of the Christian world.
        3. *Noah,* the savior of the ancient race; Christ, the Savior of all people.
        4. *The great priests of the Old Law,* who prefigured the priest of the New Law.
        5. *David,* the great king who foretold his descendant, the King of kings.
        6. *Moses,* the giver of the Ancient Law; Christ, the Giver of the New Law.
    B. The splendid figures of the *Pagan Antiquity* fade into unimportance beside the figure of Christ.
        1. The ancient *empire builders,* the Pharaohs, Xerxes, Cyrus, Alexander, Cæsar, built empires that faded from history. His empire, the Church, will exist forever.
        2. The greatest *minds of antiquity,* Socrates, Solon, Pericles, Plato, Aristotle, are still of interest largely to scholars; His mind influences the lives of countless millions.
    C. He is the *outstanding character* in all history.
        1. The influence and dominance of every other figure seems slight by comparison with Him: Augustus, Constantine, Charlemagne, Charles Martel, William the Conqueror, Charles V. Genghis Khan, Attila, Luther, Columbus, Washington, Kant, Wagner, Shakespeare, Dante, Napoleon, Lincoln, and the others.

Note: And most of these men admitted themselves His followers and believers.

D. The greatest of the *saints* is merely a reflection of one of the elements of His stature:

1. St. Paul explained His message.
2. St. Peter was His chosen representative.
3. St. Augustine restated and explained His message.
4. St. Frances, St. Dominic, St. Ignatius gathered men to serve Him more intimately and perfectly.
5. St. Francis de Sales reflected His gentleness.
6. St. Camillus of Lellis and the other lovers of mankind carried out His Beatitudes.
7. St. Thomas of Aquin wrote and taught His truths.
8. The martyrs died for love of Him.
9. The virgins were pure because of His purity.
10. The confessors strove to copy some detail of His life, His poverty, chastity, or obedience; His love of the poor; His interest in the sick.
11. The Apostles and Missionaries merely taught His message to the world.

E. *After the lapse of 1900 years,* He is the *most "alive" figure* in the world, about whom is written a constant series of best-sellers, whose story in the Gospels outsells any book or group of books ever written, and about whom today is waged the bitter fight of those who hate Him as they hate a living person and those who love Him with a love given only to the living.

Note: The modern books about Him meet astonishing popularity:

Dr. Sheldon (a Protestant) wrote *In His Steps;* and 22,000,000 copies were sold.

Bruce Barton (a Rationalist) wrote *The Man that Nobody Knows,* one of the best-sellers.

Papini's *Life of Christ* was the triumph of a literary season.

Cecil B. DeMille's film, "The King of Kings," met with widespread and enthusiastic approval.

F. *Other leaders admit His greatness:*

1. Napoleon: "Between Jesus and whomever else in the world there is no possible term of comparison."
2. Rousseau (one of the intellectual fathers of the French Revolution): "If the life and death of Socrates are those of a sage, the life and death of Jesus are those of a god."
3. Renan (father of "Modernism"): "His beauty is eternal; His reign will never end."

V. **The story of His life** is recorded in condensed form in the **Gospels.** Taking only highlights, we find:

  A. The ancient desire of mankind is satisfied. *"We will be like gods,"* all mankind had cried:

    1. Adam had sinned to obtain God's knowledge of good and evil.

    2. The pagans made their gods as human as possible so as to imitate them.

    3. All sinners have tried to steal some of God's prerogatives: His complete dominion over creatures; His right to make law; His freedom from higher authority.

    4. In the person of Jesus Christ, *"God becomes like man."* God becomes the perfect man, so that by imitating God and trying to be like the God-man, man may save himself.

  B. Christ leads a *life of perfect approachableness.*

    1. The doors of Bethlehem's stable are open to all, shepherds, wise men, travelers, the rich, the poor.

    2. The little house of Nazareth is a workshop where men can come to have small jobs done; yokes for their oxen; chairs for their homes; small toys for their children.

    3. In His public life, He is in the midst of people available to:

      a) The sick along the road.

      b) The hungry who need food.

      c) Those asking for truth.

      d) Mothers for their children.

      e) The learned, even when they came, like Nicodemus, at night.

    4. He dies on a high hill where all can see Him, with arms outstretched to welcome all mankind.

Note: In the tabernacle, He continues this perfect approachableness, waiting for all the world.

  C. *His physical appearance* is strong, robust, handsome, manly.

    1. He is "the most beautiful of the sons of men," who exercises an instant attraction upon all who meet him.

    2. He is physically strong:

      a) Trained in the hard craft of carpentry.

      b) Able to impress strong sailors and fishermen and soldiers.

      c) Able to walk thirty miles a day.

d) Capable of the tremendous work of the Public Life.

e) After the scourging, still able to carry the cross to Calvary.

3. Sunbrowned and tanned from exposure and an outdoor life.

D. *His mind is unique:*

1. In its *strength:* No body of doctrines in the world remotely approach His in universal application, variety, extent.

Note: The *Summa* of St. Thomas of Aquin is fundamentally only an extension and explanation of His teachings. All the thinkers since His day have not begun to exhaust the possibilities of His doctrines.

2. In its *delicacy and refinement:* The parables are a poet's summary and condensation of deep truths; His sermons are packed with deep thought richly imaged and expressed.

3. In its *appreciation of common problems* and the mind of the ordinary man. He draws His figures of speech from the things about Him: fields, hillside, sea, common occupations, the signs in the heavens, the instincts of human beings.

4. The simplest and most ignorant find they can follow His teaching, though the most learned and brilliant cannot exhaust its depths of meaning.

E. His *human courage* is inspiring:

1. He drives the buyers and sellers out of the temple, though alone, surrounded by the priests who hate Him, and the armed guards posted to capture Him.

2. He defends a sinful woman though He risks being stoned to death.

3. He returns from safe seclusion in Bethany to give Himself up to die.

4. At the judgment seat, He tells the truth, that He is the Son of God, knowing that this will mean His death.

5. He goes through the Passion without a cry for pity or a single sign of cowardice.

F. Coupled with this is His *wonderful gentleness:*

1. Toward His friends, Lazarus, the penitent Peter, the traitorous Judas, the cowardly Apostles.

2. Toward any stranger who came asking for a miracle; e.g., the unknown centurion, the family of the dead little girl, the widow of Naim.

3. Toward children, even when He is deeply tired.

4. Toward women, the bad as well as the good.

G. And a powerful *fascination for people:*

1. Men follow Him and become His disciples in answer to a call.

2. Five thousand men and women followed Him for three days and nights forgetful of their need for food.

3. Even the spies of the High Priest returned to report only this: "No man ever spoke as this man spoke."

H. He experiences *every type of human experience:*

1. *Poverty:* In the crib, throughout His life, in His boyhood home; "the Son of Man hath no place to lay His head"; in positive hunger; on a deathbed of planks; in a grave borrowed from a stranger.

2. *Association with all classes:*

   a) The illiterate: Constantly in childhood and youth and later among the poor of Jerusalem.

   b) The day laborers: As a carpenter, He found them His constant companions. Later He chose them for disciples.

   c) Men of the sea: From among whom He chose His Apostles.

   d) Soldiers: Who listened to Him, came to Him as did the Centurion, accepted His faith, as did the other Centurion under the cross.

   e) Members of the learned bodies: Joseph of Arimathea, Nicodemus, the scribes and Pharisees.

   f) Women: Sinful women who found Him their refuge; good women who followed and served His disciples.

   g) Rulers: Herod the Elder, and Herod who mocked Him; Pilate the Roman governor.

   h) Men of wealth: Zaccheus.

3. *Temptation:*

   a) Bodily, in the moment of hunger.

   b) Pride, from the pinnacle of the temple.

   c) Ambition, with the promise of the whole world.

   (1) These were offered by the devil empowered actually to lay physical hands upon Him.

4. *Death* of those dear to Him:

   a) The Holy Innocents.

b) Joseph, His foster father.

c) Lazarus.

5. *Separation.*

   a) From His country, during exile in Egypt.

   b) From His home, during His public life.

   c) From His mother, in the separation in the temple, and when He went out to start His mission.

6. *Ingratitude:*

   a) The recipients of His miracles failed to thank Him or later believe in Him.

   b) His disciples, when He needed them, fled away, denied Him, betrayed Him.

7. *Misunderstanding:*

   a) His relatives, when He began to preach and work His miracles, treated Him as insane.

   b) His enemies called Him a devil and in league with Satan.

   c) The priests branded Him as an imposter and a deceiver of the people.

   d) His own Apostles almost to the end of His stay on earth failed to understand His real mission.

8. *Obscurity* from birth to the beginning of His public life.

9. *Labor:*

   a) As an apprentice carpenter.

   b) As Joseph's assistant.

   c) As the sole support of His widowed mother.

10. *Sin:* but only in some of its effects:

    a) With the clear-eyed vision of its consequences to the world.

    b) In the vision of Gethsemane.

    c) From the cross when He saw its consequences in the murder of God.

11. *Failure:* Looking down from the cross He saw after three years of miracles and preaching and teaching:

    a) His disciples in hiding.

    b) His chosen people crying out for His death.

    c) The world He had come to save leagued against Him.

    d) Those who had received His favors apathetic and uninterested in this crime against Him.

12. He experienced the most beautiful of human *joys:*

a) Love for His Mother.

b) The shelter of a poor but peaceful and beautiful home.

c) The companionship of people He loved.

d) Entertainment in the homes and at the tables of people who loved Him.

e) The confidence and trust of women.

f) The love of little children.

g) The friendship with men.

h) Joy in work.

i) Realization that He was doing His Father's will.

VI. **This wonderful person** *shares His work with mankind.*

A. He invites us *to pray for the success* of His Father's Kingdom. "Thy Kingdom come, Thy will be done on earth as it is in heaven." "Pray you therefore the Lord of the harvest that He send laborers into His vineyard."

B. He invited *a special group* to be His disciples, and prepared for their successors who were to carry on His work and theirs. He promised their successors the same reward that He offered to His disciples. "Whosoever shall . . . follow Me, a hundred-fold in this life and life everlasting."

C. His followers are to *carry on the work He began,* acting through His Church.

D. All good men and women *actively advance His cause* and the kingdom of His Father. All evil men and women retard its prog-ress or actively and effectively stop its advance.

VII. Now **the educated Catholic** realizes that **This Wonderful Person,** the God-man, the dominating figure in history, the world's greatest man:

A. *Established the religion* that is Catholic, referred to it con-stantly as His Church, and gave it all its powers and authority.

B. Gave us all our *most difficult and important doctrines:*

1. The Blessed Trinity.

2. The certainty of heaven and hell.

3. The infallibility and authority of the Church.

4. The importance of human souls.

Etc., etc.

C. Laid upon us our *most difficult laws.*

1. The law of personal purity.

2. The laws against divorce and regarding marriage.

3. The relative unimportance of all the wealth in the world compared to the winning of eternal life.

4. The need of prayer and penance.

5. Forgiveness of enemies.

6. Kindness toward all men, especially the poor.

Etc., etc.

VIII. Hence, the educated Catholic makes his **religion less a matter of obedience** to blind duty or loyalty to a distinguished institution as service, personal and spontaneous, of the world's most distinguished person, an acceptance of the leadership of Jesus Christ.

Problems and Discussions

1. Explain why you think it wise or unwise for the New Law to be established on the person of Christ rather than on ideals of abstract duty.

2. How can you account for the success of such books as deal with the life of Christ?

3. If a non-Catholic said that Christians worship an effeminate and weak Christ, what could you answer?

4. Compare Christ with the other famous religious leaders: Confucius, Mohammed, Buddha, Krishna. In what elements does the comparison quickly fail?

5. What should be the natural inclination and reaction of any intelligent and decent person who knew that:

   a) By being deeply and consistently good he was advancing the cause of Jesus Christ?

   b) By being and doing evil he was spoiling, as far as he could, the work of Jesus Christ?

6. Indicate to a non-Catholic how Christ is the central figure of history, even if He were not the God-man.

7. A non-Christian asks: "Why do you follow a leader who has been dead for 1900 years?" What would you answer?

8. What qualities of mind and heart and body make Christ an inevitable leader?

9. Can God safely say to mankind of the present: "Now you may strive to be and have every ambition to become like God."

10. Give instances from the Gospel history of Christ's:

    a) Approachableness.

    b) Understanding of human problems.

c) Powerful yet delicate mind.
d) Physical strength.
e) Appeal for all classes.

11. A great leader never says, "Go, and I will approve you"; but, "Come, follow me." Show in view of this that Christ is a great leader.
12. Mention some of Christ's human relationships that seem to you particularly inspiring.
13. Why can it be said of Christ that He, beyond all others, was all things to all men?
14. Is there something inspiring in the fact that Christ has shared His work with His followers? Explain.
15. Explain to a non-Catholic why to an educated Catholic religion means doing what Christ asks and commands, and why that is splendid and inspiring.
16. Indicate briefly how Christ is the author or teacher of the main truths of the Catholic Faith, and the chief source of its difficult laws. What difference should this make in the attitude of an intelligent man?
17. Read one of the Gospels through, by preference at one sitting, seeing its interest, story value, charm, gripping power.

Suggested Readings

PAMPHLETS

The Queen's Work Press:
Christ the Modern, Lord, S.J.
Christ and Women, Lord, S.J.
The Man We Can't Ignore, Walker, S.J.
America Press:
Christ the King, Husslein, S.J.
Christ and Mankind, Scott.
Christ True God, Scott.
The Catholic Truth Society:
The Divinity of Christ, Gillis, C.S.P.
Jesus Christ is God, Courbet.

BOOKS

Marmion, *Christ the Life of the Soul* (Herder).
Adams, *Christ Our Brother* (Macmillan).
Benson, *The Friendship of Christ* (Longmans).
Filion, *Life of Christ* (Herder).
Fouard, *Christ the Son of God* (Longmans).
Goodier, *The Public Life of Jesus Christ* (Kenedy).
Plus, *Christ in His Brethren* (Benziger).
McCabe, *Ecce Homo* (Bruce).

Chapter XXI

THE LIVING AND PRESENT CHRIST

I. **Jesus Christ** could be regarded:

A. *As a magnificent historical person* whose influence has extended and endured over twenty centuries.

B. *As the Risen Christ* whose living spirit broods over the world, while He Himself is only physically present at the right hand of His Father in heaven.

C. *As the Eucharistic Christ* who is "Emmanuel," "God With Us," and who will be with His creatures until the end of time.

D. To the historian, who is not a Christian, Christ is the first.

E. To the Christian, who is not a Catholic, Christ is the first and second.

F. To the Catholic, Christ is all three.

II. **The Last Supper** was deeply significant and the precisely appropriate time *for the institution of the Blessed Sacrament:*

A. Judas had already sold Christ to His enemies, and the betrayal was set for that night.

B. As night drew on, the Roman soldiers were detailed to help make the arrest.

C. As the supper was being prepared, the High Priests were laying their final plans, guards were being assigned:

   1. To capture and destroy Christ.

   2. By a death so terrible that:

     a) It was reserved for slaves or the lowest criminals.

     b) It was regarded as the utmost disgrace.

     c) Because of it no one would again dare to admit he was a follower of a discredited, crucified leader.

D. Christ chose this night to thwart the plans of His enemies who had determined to slay Him and obliterate His name, by a counterplan to remain with the world forever:

   1. By instituting the Blessed Sacrament, His real and continued physical presence in the midst of mankind.

III. **Preparations for the Institution:**
    A. To prove *His power over the elements* of the Blessed Sacrament (bread and wine):
       1. Christ multiplied five loaves of *bread* to feed 5,000 people. (He was to multiply the new Bread of Life to feed the world of His followers.)
       2. He changed water into *wine*.
       (This was a preliminary step to changing wine into His blood.)
    B. The Blessed Sacrament was the fulfillment of the prophetic "type" of the Manna, the Heavenly Bread given the faithful journeying in the desert. This was the real Heavenly Bread given the faithful journeying toward heaven.
    C. He had *promised that He would do this,* in the most precise and careful words, and did so after He had prepared the minds of men for the idea of the Blessed Sacrament by multiplying the loaves and fishes. (St. John, Chapter VI.)

IV. He then *instituted the Blessed Sacrament* as the means of **leaving His real, physical presence** in the world.

Note: As this will be treated fully later on in the religious course, the present we simply notice:

1. That *His words were absolutely clear:* "This is My body; this is My blood."
2. He ordered *His disciples to continue* to do what He was doing.
3. *St. Paul repeating the scene,* said that it was being reënacted by the Christians of his day, and that any man who received the Eucharist unworthily was "guilty of the body and blood of Christ."
4. *All the Churches,* true and false, except the Protestants, believe in the Blessed Sacrament. (And among the Protestants, the High Episcopalians believe in it.)
5. *From the very beginning of Christianity,* we have the clearest proofs that the Christians believed this.
    A. Hence, *Christ has not left us;* He is present in Holy Communion and on our altars; and He stays with us for our sakes and to supply us with the present leadership we need.
    B. After **Jansenism,** out of a false idea of reverence for God, kept Christians from receiving the Blessed Sacrament frequently, **Pius X** gave back **frequent Communion** to the world:

    1. Because Christ wanted this.

    2. Because in early pagan days (in many ways much like the present pagan days) when persecution was rife and dangers common, the Christians received daily or at least always frequent Communion.

    3. Because the men and women of our age, the young men and women especially, need frequent Communion.

Note: There are two versions of the Our Father:

    1. "Give us this day our daily bread."
    2. "Give us this day our supersubstantial bread."

Thus the evangelists indicated that the supersubstantial bread, the Blessed Sacrament, was to be daily as was the bread upon our tables.

IV. **What happens in Holy Communion,** in the receiving of the Blessed Sacrament?

    A. One of His followers enters into the most *intimate and beautiful relationship* with Christ.

    B. Christ *supplies for his weakness and limitations* by giving:

        1. His *strength* for the man's weakness.

        2. His *purity* against the man's temptations.

        3. His *divine life* to supplement the man's human life.

        4. His *courage* to fortify the man's cowardice.

    C. He further incorporates the communicant into *His own Mystical Body.*

        1. Christ is the *head* of that Body.

        2. The communicant becomes more completely one *member* of the Body.

        3. He is thus *united with Christ* and with other Catholics who, through Holy Communion, have become more completely members of the Mystical Body of Christ.

Note: This is treated at length later in the religion course.

    D. Christ so *associates Himself* with all those who receive:

        1. That they are more completely one in His Mystical Body.

        2. And the Heavenly Father sees and approves this union.

V. **The effects** of this are:

    A. Great stores of *divine grace* are received by the communicant from the very source of grace, Jesus Christ Himself.

B. New *strength* is gained against temptation.

C. New *courage* is acquired for the battle of life.

D. Opportunity is given for *personal consultation* with the Leader.

Note: St. Paul believed the Blessed Sacrament *the great safeguard against impurity.* He felt that one who received worthily could not "take the body of Christ and give it to harlots," i.e., could not take his own body to which Christ's body had been united and which was now part of the Mystical Body of Christ and give it to impurity.

The Saints call the Blessed Sacrament:

1. *The Bread of Angels,* i.e., bread that makes men like those who have no bodies to be tempted and defiled.

2. *The wine that produces virgins,* i.e., where ordinary wine inflames the passions, this wine develops purity.

VI. For a college student:

A. Surrounded by temptations against purity.

B. Beset by books and articles attacking faith.

C. In need of divine light and strength to do well in studies.

D. Trying to form habits for life.

E. In need of a Leader whose consultation and advice and guidance can be trusted;

1. *Weekly communion* should be the personal practice of all.

2. *Daily communion* should be the ideal and aspiration.

3. *Monthly communion* should be the absolute minimum.

Note: If temptations and needs are daily, the strength against them must be daily supplied.

VII. The student will receive from Holy Communion grace and strength in proportion to the **preparation** and **thanksgiving** he makes.

A. **Preparation:**

1. *Freedom from mortal sin* is essential.

   a) This means that one must go to confession if there is any serious sin.

   b) If there is no serious sin, confession at least once in two weeks is advised.

2. *Fasting from midnight* is, of course, the law of the Church.

Note: The fast is only broken by what is consumed as food or drink; hence, nothing but real food or drink can break a fast.

3. *Before receiving Holy Communion,* the person should prepare his soul:

 a) By hearing Mass intelligently and well, realizing that his communion is part of the Mass.

 (This is the desire of Christ, who made Communion part of the Mass; and it is the ideal method.)

 b) By thinking quietly over what is to occur and planning the interview with the Leader.

 c) By acts of faith, hope, love, sorrow for sin. These may be taken either from one's prayer book or from one's heart.

B. **Thanksgiving:**

Note: Christ is physically present at least for 10 minutes and probably for 15 minutes after receiving.

1. The one who has received may:

 a) Recite the official prayers said by the priest. These are found in every *Missal.*

 b) Talk quietly with Christ:

 (1) Expressing gratitude for this Communion and for the many blessings and favors of a lifetime.

 (2) Discussing problems, difficulties, and needs.

 (3) Praying for special persons or special intentions.

 (4) Thinking of Christ as: The Babe of Bethlehem; the Carpenter and Friend of the poor; the great Teacher; the suffering Savior.

 (5) Speaking to Him as a devoted follower to his leader.

 (6) Using the thanksgiving prayers in the prayer book.

 (7) Freely pouring out our Love to Him.

VIII. During the day, Christ remains in the tabernacle. Hence, to gain strength and grace:

 A. **Short Visits to the Blessed Sacrament** are important and precious:

 1. Especially between classes.

 2. Before big events, such as games, parties, debates, etc.

 3. In time of need for self and others.

 Refer back to Chapter XVII.

IX. *We follow a Leader who remains with us,* waiting on our desires and needs, ready for consultation, guidance, help; and eager to give us strength, courage, purity, knowledge.

Problems and Discussions

1. Explain to a non-Catholic why Jesus Christ is so vivid in the consciousness of an intelligent Catholic.
2. Explain to a non-Catholic the way in which Christ prepared the minds of His followers for the institution of the Blessed Sacrament.
3. If the Jews had the Manna and the Christians had not received the Blessed Sacrament, do you feel that the New Law would be in that respect inferior to the Old? Give your reasons. Compare the Manna with the Blessed Sacrament in its characteristics, effects, etc.
4. Explain the statement: "Either the Blessed Sacrament is the Body and Blood of Christ, or Christ is responsible for countless sins of idolatry."
5. Does frequent Communion seem to be particularly important in this generation? Give reasons for your answer. Do our times suggest the pagan days of Rome and the consequent need of frequent Communion?
6. Explain these expressions used of the Blessed Sacrament:
    a) This is the Bread of the strong.
    b) This is the true Staff of Life.
    c) This is the wine that makes virgins.
    d) In the strength of this food you shall walk to the mountain of God.
7. Can you give an explanation of why Christ chose bread and wine as the elements of the Blessed Sacrament when He might have chosen other things instead?
8. A student says: "I am frightfully tempted and fall into sin again and again. I don't see why I am so weak when I go to Communion twice a year." Discuss the statement with him.
9. Discuss this advice of a priest: "If you and the young lady you go with find each other sources of temptation, go to Holy Communion together."
10. Discuss the relative grace that will be received under the following conditions: The person:
    a) Arrives at the Communion of the Mass and goes immediately to Holy Communion.
    b) Reads a chapter of the Fourth Book of Thomas à Kempis.
    c) Dreams through Mass.
    d) Reads his Missal and pays special attention to those prayers of the priest before Holy Communion.
    e) Says his rosary.
    f) Meditates on the Last Supper and imagines himself one of the Disciples.

11. Discuss the following actions as thanksgivings after Communion. The person:
    a) Leaves the church at the last blessing.
    b) Stays for ten minutes but as he has not prepared for this, he finds at the end of the time that he has done nothing.
    c) Says the Litany of the Blessed Virgin.
    d) Says the Litany of the Holy Name.
    e) Thanks our Savior for three things; asks Him for three things; promises Him three things; and discusses three things with Him.
    f) Reads from a prayer book the prayers after Communion.
    g) Says the prayers assigned to a priest to recite after Mass.
12. Discuss this statement: "Men would have forgotten very much about Christ had He not stayed on in the Blessed Sacrament."
13. Discuss this statement: "In instituting the Blessed Sacrament, Christ acted with a divine love, a human wisdom, and a deep regard for our needs."
14. Can Holy Communion be properly called "Consultation with my Leader"?

Suggested Readings

PAMPHLETS

The Queen's Work Press:
Christ Lives On, Lord, S.J.
A Traveler in Disguise, Lord, S.J.
The Paulist Press:
Holy Communion — in the Gospels, Hedley.
Holy Communion in the Early Church, Hedley.
America Press:
The Eucharist, Husslein, S.J.
The Catholic Truth Society:
The Real Presence, Mangan.
See *Catholic Encyclopedia:* "Eucharist"; "Holy Communion"; "Blessed Sacrament"; *et passim.*

Chapter XXII

A HEAVENLY MOTHER

I. **Every successful man or woman** recognizes with the passing of years **his debt to his mother.** As the Gracchi did to Cornelia; Louis of France to Queen Blanche; St. Augustine to St. Monica; Abraham Lincoln to Nancy Hanks; and a thousand similar instances.

II. **Love of Mother** is:
   A. The most *fundamental* of human emotions.
   B. Inspiring the *loveliest tributes of art;* e.g., the Madonnas.
   C. Awakening a never-ending *flow of literature;* e.g., most authors dedicate their first books to their mothers.
   D. Emotionally so *universal in appeal* that it reappears in the most popular types of song and verse.
   E. For men and women realize with advancing years:
   a) The debt of *birth* owed to a mother.
   b) The patient *care* that surrounded infancy.
   c) The early *training* for life that was largely given by her.
   d) The *hope for the future* that filled her heart for her children.
   e) Her *confidence* that grew and continued despite disappointments and failures.
   f) Her unfailing *sympathy* and quick understanding.

Hence an adult woman, especially after marriage, often grows closer to and more appreciative of her mother.

An adult man comes to know that if he succeeds in life, he is only realizing a part of his mother's hopes and dreams for him.

III. The instinct of love for mother is closely *linked with the instinct for religion:*
   A. Because *mothers are usually the first and natural teachers* of religion and morality.
   B. Because the *goodness and unselfishness of a mother* and her love suggests the great goodness and love of God for His children.

IV. **Christ, who** had no father save God, **deliberately chose to have a mother:**

    A. *Who bore Him* at the cost of painful suspicion on the part of Joseph, a long and wearisome journey to Bethlehem, and the deep poverty of the stable.

    B. Who gave Him all the *faithful service and personal care* a mother gives her infant and growing son.

    C. Who, after the death of Joseph, became *dependent upon Him* for her support. He worked as a carpenter to earn her food and housing. She cared for His house and prepared His food in return.

    D. Who, like a devoted mother, *obliterated herself,* during the days of His success and public life.

    E. But who *reappeared at the time of His rejection* and apparent failure to be near Him in His death agony.

    F. Upon whom *He sent the Holy Ghost* as He did to His disciples.

    G. Hence, Christ bore to His mother the same relationship that fine sons bear to their mother, plus a divine gratitude.

        1. He accepted gratefully her service of Him.

        2. He was her sole support for years.

        3. He worked the first miracle in advance of His appointed time because she asked it.

V. **Mary,** however, was more than any other mother that had lived:

    A. She was the *mother of a divine Person,* the Second Person of the Blessed Trinity, Jesus Christ, God and man.

    B. Though she was mother of the human nature (not the divine) she was mother of the divine Person who possessed both natures. Hence, she was **the Mother of God.**

Note: Every mother is *the mother of a complete person,* who possesses a body and a soul; even though she is directly responsible for the production of the body and not the soul, she is still the mother, not of the body, but of the complete human person.

So Mary is the *mother of a complete divine person* who is God; and though she is directly responsible for the production of the human nature and not of the divine nature, she is the mother of the complete person, who is God. Hence, she is the mother of God.

    C. *Her free consent,* when the Angel Gabriel consulted her, meant the beginning of the Incarnation.

D. She was *present at the essential events* in the life of Christ, coöperating thus in the redemption of mankind:

1. The *Incarnation* waited upon her consent.
2. The *Nativity* found her the chief figure.
3. The *flight into Egypt* was her means of saving the life of Christ.
4. The *hidden life* of 30 years was lived in her home.
5. The *public life* began with the miracle worked at her request.
6. On *Calvary,* the sword, prophesied by Simeon in the temple, pierced her heart. She became with Christ the victim of our sins. She united her agony of soul with His agony of body.

E. Hence **she coöperated** as no other creature did **in the redemptive work of Christ for men.**

VI. **The Catholic Church** has wisely and with divine inspiration known that:

A. Because He was a good son, Christ would always be eager to do as His mother desired.

1. Hence, she would be *powerful in her requests to Him.*

B. Because she knew from experience the poverty, sufferings, needs and troubles of mankind, she would be quick to ask grace and favors for human beings.

1. Hence, she would be a *willing intercessor for men.*

C. Because Christ actually gave mankind from His deathbed of the cross His mother to be our mother too, she would be *keenly interested in us.*

1. John beneath the cross represented mankind when Christ said: "Son, behold thy mother."

D. The Apostles fled to Mary immediately after the death of her Son and remained with her during the days of uncertainty and peril until the descent of the Holy Ghost.

1. Always she remained *the Queen of the Apostles,* interested in the salvation of souls for which her Son had died.

E. While Christ taught us to regard God as our Father, He wisely knew our love of and need for a mother too, and so He gave us His own mother as **our Heavenly Mother.**

VII. **History** from the very first has shown that this was the attitude of the whole Christian world.

Note: Not till Protestantism arose in the sixteenth century was this honor denied to Mary. During the Reformation her statues were broken, her altars and shrines smashed, her name stricken from the prayer books, as if a great Son could be honored by dishonoring His mother.

A. *Every saint* has shown the most tender and filial love for Mary.

    1. From St. John, who cared for her till her death and St. Luke, who reproduced her story in his Gospel.

    2. Through the saints who dedicated their lives and religious orders to her: St. Benedict, St. Bernard, St. Dominic, the seven saintly founders of the Servants of Mary, the saintly founders of the Order of Our Lady of Mercy for the Redemption of Captives, etc.

    3. To the most modern saints, each one of whom has been characterized by a deep love of Mary: The Curé of Ars, the Little Flower, Father Chaminade, founder of the Society of Mary, and all others.

B. From the beginning *Christian art* has been filled with tributes to her: from the madonna attributed to St. Luke, through the early mosaics and statues, to the glorious paintings of the golden era of the Renaissance.

C. Her *hymns and prayers* fill the liturgy of the Church:

    1. The Hail Mary, composed by the Angel Gabriel, St. Elizabeth, and the first ages of the Church.

    2. The *Magnificat,* Mary's own beautiful prayer.

    3. The *Angelus,* said during the Middle Ages as a protection against the Turk.

    4. The *Stabat Mater,* called by some the greatest poem of a thousand years.

    5. The *Litany,* compiled from the age-old titles used to honor her.

    6. The *Memorare,* beloved prayer of St. Bernard.

D. *Countries have been dedicated* to her:

    1. England, called the Dowery of Mary.

    2. America, dedicated to the Immaculate Conception.

    3. France, Italy, and Spain, whose famous shrines and greatest cathedrals are under her patronage.

E. The succession of her *feasts* fill the year, from that of her Nativity to that of her Assumption into heaven.

F. She has been regarded with the deepest love:

    1. By mothers, who saw in her the perfect mother.

2. By young men, who tried to live up to what their Heavenly Mother hoped of them.

3. By young women, who remembered her virginity that drew God Himself down from heaven.

4. By all good men, who respected women because of her.

5. By all good women who respected themselves because of their likeness to her.

VIII. **The attitude of a Catholic student** toward Mary must be:

A. The devoted *love of a son or daughter* for a mother who is powerful with Christ, her eldest son, and who is deeply interested in her younger children.

B. *Showing itself:*

1. In instinctive *honor* paid to that mother:

   a) Through membership in her Sodality.

   b) Through daily prayers to her: An attentive *angelus;* a daily Rosary; Prayers to her upon rising for protection and at retiring in thanksgiving; ejaculations in time of peril or temptation.

2. Special regard for May and October and for her feast days.

3. In a generous *imitation of her life.* Realizing that they are her children they must reflect in their lives:

   a) Her love of her son, Jesus Christ.

   b) Her spotless purity.

   c) Her devotion to her home.

   d) Her deep respect for womanhood.

IX. **This attitude** of the student shows itself:

A. In his *devotional life.* Often prayer to Mary is easy when no other prayer will be. Often when shame for sin holds the student back from Christ, trust in a mother's understanding and love makes prayer to Mary inevitable.

B. In his *social life.* One's social life more than anything else reflects:

1. The type of family from which one comes.

2. One's own personal ideals, desires, and interests.

The Catholic student knows he comes of a family whose Mother is Mary and whose oldest Son is Jesus Christ.

He knows that a child of such a family must have high ideals and interests.

X. Hence, a son or daughter of Mary will lead a **Social Life:**

    A. In which *no sin can have part.*

        1. Aside from the fact that sin leads to headache, heartache, regret, and remorse, he will not lower the dignity of his "family relation" with sinful amusements.

    B. In which the young men realize that *they must pay proper respect* to the young women, because they are the daughters of the same Mother. And the young women respect themselves, as they are the daughters of a virgin Mother.

Note: The Catholic student feels that he carries the reputation of his Mother with him into his social life.

    C. In the *personal purity* of the student.

Note: This is discussed in the following chapter.

    D. In a genuine *interest in the home.*

Note: No finer way can be found for honoring Mary than by honoring **one's own Mother and Father:**

1. Who have made tremendous sacrifices for the student's sake.
2. Who depend more than the student is aware on him or her for their happiness.

This interest is shown:

1. By *cheerfulness* around the house.
2. By a *respect* for the rights of younger brothers and sisters.
3. By a *cheerful deference* to the wishes as well as to the positive commands of parents.
4. By willingly *performing such duties* of the home as are intrusted to the student.

Problems and Discussions

1. Answer the following statement: "The honor Catholics pay to Mary detracts from the honor due to Christ."
2. Answer this common Protestant argument: "Mary is the mother of Jesus Christ, the man; but she could not be and is not the mother of God."
3. Is it true or false that a nation does not rise above the moral level of its mothers? Give reasons for your answer.
4. Show why it is religiously fitting that we have a Heavenly Mother.
5. Is this argument valid: "If Christ did not love and honor His mother, He would not have been a good man"?

6. Does the Catholic Church regard the Blessed Virgin as a goddess?
7. Indicate Mary's share in the redemptive work of her Son.
8. What are some important reasons why Catholics think Mary must be powerful in her intercession with her Son?
9. If the saints consistently honored Mary, what would you have said to the sixteenth-century reformer denouncing Mary?
10. List some famous Madonnas. Some famous shrines of Mary. Some prayers to her not listed in the chapter.
11. A Catholic student is by faith and usually by consecration a child of Mary. In view of this fact, discuss the following possible actions:
    a) A plays ball all through the ringing of the college *angelus*.
    b) B always tries to find out how far he can go with the girls he takes out.
    c) C, a Catholic girl, gets giddily drunk at a party and acts like a fool.
    d) D (boy or girl) is quite willing to help with the care of the home and does so during the holidays.
    e) E says the beads daily, usually going home on the bus.
    f) F has a statue of Mary on his (or her) dresser.
    g) G admits that when she goes out she freely "necks."
    h) H in a non-Catholic group tells off-color stories.
    i) I always refers to his (or her) mother as "the old lady."
    j) J says the *Memorare* every evening before retiring.
    k) K cynically declares that all girls are "soft and easy."
    l) L, a college girl, acts in a way to justify K's cynicism.
    m) M dresses like a chorus girl.
    n) N dresses in correct fashion, but avoids the two extremes of dowdiness and flashiness.
12. Your roommate asks you what prayers you think a college student should recite to our Lady.
13. A student says, "I say three Hail Marys at night; so I can go ahead and sin. The Blessed Virgin will take care of me."
14. Prove to a non-Catholic that devotion to the Blessed Virgin is an important element in the life of a right-minded college student.

Suggested Readings

PAMPHLETS

The Queen's Work Press:
  When Mary Walked the Earth, Lord, S.J.
  The Months with Mary, Lord, S.J.
The Paulist Press:
  Mary Mother of God, Sheehan.
America Press:

The Blessed Virgin, Husslein, S.J.
All Grace Through Mary, Husslein, S.J.
Mary Immaculate, Lonergan, S.J.
The Catholic Truth Society:
Life of the Blessed Virgin, Vassall-Phillips.

BOOKS

Maxwell, *Mary, the Mother of Jesus* (Medici Society).
Stourton, *Regina Poetarum* (Washbourne).
Ligouri, *The Glories of Mary* (McVey).
See the *Catholic Encyclopedia:* "Blessed Virgin"; "Mary"; *et passim.*

Chapter XXIII

PURITY

I. **The Catholic college student** is:
  A. A professed follower of the *pure Christ*.
  B. A child of the *Immaculate Virgin Mother*.
  C. A younger brother or sister of the *saints*.
  D. Fed by the *pure body and blood of Christ* in the Blessed Sacrament.
  E. Hence, he or she must by force of heredity and environment **be pure.**

II. *The struggle to preserve their purity* is the common struggle of all decent young people; because:
  A. **Purity** is something so *very important and very beautiful* that it deserves a struggle.
  B. During youth there comes the *physical transition* through which a child becomes an adult; and the physical transition means the maturing and sudden awakening with the consequent sharp consciousness of the powers of sex.
  C. Because of this, **temptations** are inevitable, often frequent, and sometimes violent. But they are shared alike by all young people in whom the fact of temptation is merely a proof that they are physically normal.
    1. These temptations include:
      a) *Mental temptations:* Impulses toward thoughts and emotions and desires usually connected with persons of the opposite sex.
      b) *Physical temptations:* Impulses within the individual toward actions which conscience assures the individual are wrong.
      c) *Social temptations:* Impulses toward conduct while in the company of others that conscience indicates to be low or common or positively evil:
        (1) Improper *conversation*.
        (2) Improper *intimacies* between the sexes.
        (3) Improper *actions* when in the company of others.

III. **Purity** must be regarded *not as a negative thing.* This would be to define purity as "the absence of impurity," which is simply the "noncommission of improper actions." Purity is *one of the strongest and most positive of virtues,* safeguarding the powers upon which depend the whole future of the race and usually the future happiness of the individual.

In addition, every young man or woman knows the *courage necessary* to say "No" to temptation and to keep up the constant warfare necessary to repel the attacks of temptation from within and without.

IV. **God shares with human beings His best powers:**
  A. *Intellect:* So that men can know truth and eventually can know God Himself.
  B. *Free Will:* So that men act not as animals act by force of brute instinct, but as God acts, freely and with deliberation. Man is free to act or not to act, to love good and hate evil.
  C. *The power of creation:* God, the Father and Creator of the world, possesses the power of making human beings. Instead of creating them without help, He shares with men and women this power of making other human beings. This power is exercised through sex and its generative organs.

V. Hence, **the powers of sex** *are noble and splendid and deeply important,* not cheap and common and vile as modern paganism regards them.
  A. They are mankind's *sharing of God's paternity.* Men and women become fathers and mothers of human beings.
  B. *God waits upon mankind's use* of these powers to create human souls to inform and vivify the human body. *These souls:*
    1. Will be *not merely destined for earth.*
    2. But designed for an *eternal destiny.*
    3. Through the *redemption of the Savior* and the sanctification of the Holy Spirit.
  C. *God sanctifies and blesses* these powers by the beautiful emotion known as **love.**

VI. **Love** is the permanent attraction by which a man and woman are drawn together, inclining them to join their lives in an unbreakable unity, to establish a home, and together to work out their life's destiny and to form together the basis of a family into which children will be safely and beautifully born.

Passion is often mistaken for love. Passion is not a permanent but a transient or passing attraction. It thinks only of the immediate self-gratification, has no regard for the question of unity, home, children, or the mutual working out together of life's problems and difficulties, as well as the sharing of its delights.

Passion unaccompanied by love is merely animal. Passion sanctified by love is human and approved by God.

VII. **To consecrate and safeguard this love:**
  A. *Christ raised marriage to the dignity of a Sacrament.*
  The Nuptial Mass is said for the young couple; the Eucharistic Christ is the first guest of the wedding. The sacrament gives them the special graces needed to carry out the duties and ob-bligations of their new life.
  B. God has given to *love* (*not to mere passion*) *a setting of beauty and dignity.*
   1. Men and women who really love *wish to bind themselves* in a permanent union that will last for life.

Note: While modern pagan writers try to make escape from marriage easy, all real lovers try by their vows to make this "escape" impossible.

   2. They *grow unselfish,* thinking more of the happiness of the other party than of their own.

Note: Gifts are the sign of love, the desire of the lover to be unselfish, to give rather than to take.

   3. Because of love, they:
    a) Write more *beautiful literature.*
    b) Compose more *exquisite music.*
    c) Paint finer and more *inspiring pictures.*
   4. They feel a *new ambition* that lifts them up to better and nobler achievements.

Passion, on the other hand, is usually selfish and self-centered, preferring self-gratification to the desires of the other; degrades and debases even high genius; has an animal transientness about it that today is most notable in literature and life; and very often completely spoils the whole of a life.

VIII. Upon the **proper use of the powers** of sex depend:
  A. The safe and proper and beautiful *entrance of human beings* into the world. These human beings are to be:

      1. Citizens of earth.

      2. Eternal citizens of heaven.

  B. The *unselfish and permanent love* of a man and a woman from which result:

      1. *A home* in which life is lived safely and with dignity.

      2. *Mental companionship* to supplement the physical.

      3. *Mutual coöperation* in the work of two lives united into one.

      4. Much of the world's greatest and *finest art* and literature and music.

      5. Well-directed *ambition* and achievement.

IX. Sex is sacred and important:

  A. Because *life* is sacred and important.

  B. Because *children* are the hope of the future.

  C. **Purity** is merely the splendid and brave safeguarding of sex, its great creative powers, and the important things which depend upon it.

Note: When impurity becomes common and sex is ridiculed and made the subject for dirty jokes and vulgar contempt, this is because a pagan and ignoble view is taken of life itself. Pagans who despise life as futile, laugh at sex and debase it. Christians who regard life as sacred and beautiful, revere and reverence and safeguard sex because sex is the gateway of life.

X. Today the **college man and woman** live surrounded by a contempt for sex based on *a pagan contempt for life:*

  A. The best-selling *novels and plays* applaud the heroes and heroines who defy the laws safeguarding sex.

  B. The "free soul" (who is usually free from morality and often common decency) is the approved soul.

  C. The *revues and stage sketches* laugh at sex and its violations as vulgar, amusing, common, funny.

  D. The *social attitudes* stimulate passion among men and women and try to instill in youthful minds the idea that passion is more important than love.

      1. They encourage young men and women to *a stimulation of passion and a simulation of love* with every chance companion of an afternoon or evening.

      2. They keep insisting that *youth cannot be pure* and hence is foolish to try.

3. They *feed passion with exciting liquor* which often inflames passion beyond control.

4. *Philosophically* stating that men are the same as beasts, they encourage them to act as beasts.

5. Young women are told that they most easily *buy popularity* by sexual intimacies or emotional carelessness that imperils their own future and the future of their children yet unborn.

6. Young men are told that they must and may find *sexual license* wherever they can.

E. *A low and contemptuous attitude toward marriage* is taken. It is treated as a transient union, entered casually, and broken on slight provocation; with almost no regard for its relation to children, home, the finer arts, ambition, the sharing of difficulties, problems, anxieties, joys.

XI. Yet these young men and women to whom this lax and purely animal sex immorality is preached:

A. Will be the *fathers and mothers* of the future.

What sort of mothers and fathers will they be if they contaminate the sources of life by impurity and take this contemptuous attitude toward the means of bringing children into the world?

B. Later they hope to find a *love that will satisfy them* for life and result in a permanent union with splendid consequences for their life.

But this free exercise of passion makes difficult if not absolutely impossible the existence later of real love. The constant imitation of love through passion destroys the power of genuine love. With this gone, the beautiful consequences cannot follow.

C. Later they must bring to the person they really hope to love (and perhaps actually do love):

1. *A soiled body.*

2. *A shopworn emotion.*

3. Only the *same signs of love* that they have degraded and diluted and despoiled by passion indulged in with chance acquaintances.

D. They will hope to *inspire in their children* a purity that they know in their hearts they themselves did not possess.

1. Children themselves are quick to detect the insincerity of parents asking of them a purity they themselves threw away.

E. Hence, purity is merely the brave and human and splendid

safeguarding of the future of the individual and the future of the race.

Note 1: God and nature meant the *body of a woman* to be attractive to a man. But that womanly body is *sacred* because:

   a) It is the *chalice,* literally, of future life.
   b) It is the *tabernacle* in which will be housed infant humanity.
   c) It is the *fountain* of the human race.

Because of this:

   a) **Modesty** requires that it be gracefully and adequately clothed, as all sacred objects are covered.
   b) *Reverence* for its sacred character and importance demands that it be touched only with respectful hands, never by hands that will profane or despoil it.

Note 2: *The attraction between a man and a woman* is a natural and in itself a beautiful one. However, it must be controlled if it is not to degenerate into passion. It cannot be allowed to have its sway when it is directed toward a chance companion, toward a forbidden person, toward one for whom one cannot entertain the thought of marriage. Unrestrained license given to this attraction leads to promiscuity with its terrible consequences.

Note 3: *Temptations are natural* and inevitable but by no means startling or terrifying. Their presence merely indicates the development of sexual powers. They must be treated firmly, quietly, effectively, but without worry.

Note 4: Since *man is the "positive" element* or the natural leader in sex matters, and this by force of his nature and physical constitution:

   a) He naturally *proposes marriage,* which is the final and effective consecration of love.
   b) He is usually *more severely tempted.*
      (1) Hence, he must be personally more careful about avoiding temptation.
      (2) Hence, a pure girl will consider it her obligation and privilege to help him remain good. Her lesser temptations and more slowly awakened emotional nature must be a sedative and quieting influence upon him.
         It is not kind but positively cruel to a man who has any decencies left to yield to his improper advances. Kindness that remains pure will assist him to safeguard his own future and his own dignity.

Note 5: Temptation grows more *violent and more insistent when it is yielded* to or stimulated from outside.

Hence the obvious peril of:
- *a*) Improper pictures.
- *b*) Obscene stories.
- *c*) Careless physical attitudes.
- *d*) Too easy association or contact between the sexes.
- *e*) Dangerously stimulating dances.
- *f*) Seductive stage presentations.
- *g*) The use of liquor in mixed groups.

Liquor has a double effect: It highly *stimulates the passions* of a man, and it considerably *lowers the moral resistance* of a woman. People otherwise decent, under the influence of liquor find themselves violently tempted and perilously weak. This is the simple and constant experience of mankind, and is known through the sad experience of those who disregarded history's warnings.

XII. Helps to Purity:

A. A deep realization of *the beauty and importance of the creative powers* intrusted to mankind by God, the powers upon which depend so much individual happiness and so much of the future of the race. Hence the stern obligation of *safeguarding* this power.

B. *Avoidance of occasions of sin.* Good plays should be patronized. Clean books should be read. Only decent and wholesome company should be kept. In time of temptation the mind must be kept busy and cheerful.

C. *Frequent reception of the pure body of the Savior* in Holy Communion. (This has been treated in Chapter XXI.)

D. Devotion to *Our Virgin Mother.* (This has been treated in Chapter XXII.)

E. The choice of *a regular confessor* to whom the student goes frequently. Advice in this matter is most important. Regular confession is a great source of strength.

F. An attitude of *deep respect for self,* and an unobtrusive but effective insistence upon that respect from others. This respect is gained not through words but through conduct.

G. *Avoidance of intoxicants.*

Note 1: Though the world may be ever so rotten, strangely enough *it expects the Catholic young man and woman to be pure.* It is frankly shocked and scandalized when they are not.

Note 2: The Catholic young man and the Catholic young woman should *consider each has a responsibility* to and for the other. Each knows the ideals and obligations that bind both. They can be of the most powerful mutual assistance if they both determine to live up to their principles.

Note 3: The loud, boisterous, vulgar, and *dangerous party* is, as everyone knows, an immediate occasion of sin. It is not only wrong, but it is utterly unbecoming a Catholic, and below the dignity of a decent human being.

Problems and Discussions

1. Answer this statement common in modern literature: "Purity is a negative virtue, and hence weak compared with courage or other positive virtues."
2. Is this true or false: The whole safety of the future depends upon the purity of those who one day will be fathers and mothers?
3. Explain why the power of sex is a thing of dignity and sacredness.
4. What difference toward sex would you expect between a pagan who thought all men just animals, and a Catholic who thought all men to be the sons and daughters of God?
5. Is "puppy love" likely to be love or passion?
6. A man proposes to a girl he did not know before the evening began and while he is under the influence of drink and after a rough party. Should the girl feel flattered?
7. What qualities should one expect to find in real love?
8. Show that God elevated love and that true love elevates man.
9. Why does a Christian man lift his hat when he meets a woman?
10. Discuss the statement: The cheap attitude taken by films and magazines and stage and novel toward sex indicates that the modern pagan world has a deep contempt for life itself.
11. A young man makes love to every girl he goes out with. Later he wonders why the marriage he contracts seems loveless. Can you explain?
12. A girl who has allowed men sex liberties meets a fine young man who loves her and asks her to marry him. What will be her feeling regarding love and his possible children? What will be her attitude toward the men of her past?
13. Because J has temptations of thought, he feels himself to be abnormal. Talk his situation over with him.
14. Why can a modest girl be said to be a normal and natural girl? And why is immodesty against human experience, our best instincts, and nature itself?
15. In the light of this, discuss "nudism."
16. J feels it is quite all right to be sexually lax with a girl who does not object. What about his attitude?

17. What of this statement: Fortunate is the young man who has met and goes out with a girl who is wholesome, companionable, but allows him no liberties?
18. Is a girl really kind who allows liberties?
19. A student resolves not to sin, but reads all sorts of suggestive books and magazines. What are the inevitable consequences? Why?
20. A student troubled with temptation goes to you for advice. Give it to him.
21. Why are non-Catholics shocked at conduct in Catholic students which they readily condone in themselves?
22. Why does every indecent man try to get a girl to drink with him?

Suggested Readings

PAMPHLETS

The Queen's Work Press:
The Pure of Heart, Lord, S.J.
Speaking of Birth Control, Lord, S.J.
They're Married, Lord, S.J.
Marry Your Own, Lord, S.J.
America Press:
The Wedding Ring, Husslein, S.J.
The Church and Sex Problem, Tierney-Riordan.
*Training in Purity,** Mahoney, Rev. E. J., D.D.

BOOKS

Von Hildebrand, *In Defense of Purity* (Sheed and Ward).
Martindale, *The Difficult Commandment* (boys).
Martindale, *Into Their Company* (girls).
Alexander, *A Mother's Letters* (girls).
Meyer, *Helps to Purity* (boys).
Meyer, *Safeguards to Chastity* (girls).

*Especially valuable because the pamphlet gives the true meaning and application of the reply made by the Holy See in March, 1931, to the question, "Is the method known as *Sexual Education* or *Initiation* to be approved?" This reply refers to the teaching of the encyclical on *Christian Education.* The pamphlet, therefore, ought certainly to be read by the instructor.

Chapter XXIV

THE USE OF CONFESSION

I. *Christ carefully prepared His followers* for the fact of **Confession:**
    A. The non-Catholic argues today: "What man can forgive sins?"
This same question was asked of Christ. A paralytic lay before
Him; Christ said to him: "Thy sins are forgiven thee." The skep-
tics in the crowd said: "What man has power to forgive sins?"
Christ, to prove that as man He had this power, asked them: "Is
it easier to say 'Thy sins are forgiven' or 'Arise and walk'? But
in order that you may know that the Son of Man hath power on
earth to forgive sins," He cured the paralytic and *proved His
power.*
    B. Later *He delegated this power to His disciples:* "Receive ye the
Holy Ghost; whose sins you shall forgive they are forgiven; and
whose sins you shall retain they are retained."
    C. So, from the very first, *the Church forgave sins* or retained sins
where the penitent was clearly unworthy.

Note: Confession is essential because only by hearing the sins of the
penitent and his expression of sorrow can the priest know whether to forgive or retain these sins.

    The proofs for this will be discussed later in the religion course.
    D. So the power which Christ had, which He gave to His disciples
for the use of His Church and the sake of sinners, is passed on to
His priests who forgive sins: "I absolve you from your sins in the
name of the Father and of the Son and of the Holy Ghost."

II. **Confession** is not meant to be:
    A. *A burden* to the individual.
    B. *A source of annoyance* or scruple to anyone.
    C. *Nor an easy substitute* for sorrow for sins.

III. But *it is* meant to be:
    A. *A deep consolation,* since through it one is freed from the bur-
den of sin.
    B. *An opportunity for consultation,* through which one learns to

167

overcome the evil inclinations and to advance in virtue and grace more surely toward eternal life.

C. A time to take definite steps *to correct past mistakes* and to plan against their recurrence for the future.

D. *A source of sanctifying grace* and of actual graces that make one stronger against future temptations.

Note: The intelligent Catholic realizes that Confession was instituted by the loving Christ for aspiring saints and penitent sinners, for those who want to love Him more and hate sin more. There in the confessional the Catholic finds the Divine Physician, the Good Shepherd, and the Father of the Prodigal Son. The priest is His immediate representative.

IV. **A good confession** includes:

A. *A prayer to God for light* to know one's sins and grace to be sorry for them.

"My God, help me to know my sins and to be truly sorry for them from my heart."

B. *An honest examination of conscience.* One must try to recall:

1. *The lapse of time* since the last worthy confession.

   a) A worthy confession is one in which the penitent honestly confesses with sorrow the serious sins he remembers at the time and for which he receives absolution.

2. *The serious sins,* if any, of which one has been guilty. Their exact number must be recalled as far as this is possible.

   a) If the exact number cannot be recalled, one must remember approximately how often each month, each week, each day, they have been committed.

3. *Venial sins need not be told,* though some of them must be told if there is no serious sin to tell. Their exact number need not be told.

C. Real and sincere and *supernatural sorrow for sins.* This is absolutely essential and must include a firm determination with God's help not to sin seriously again.

D. *An honest recital* of these sins to the priest. His questions (if any) insofar as they regard the sins must be truthfully answered.

E. *The penance* given by the priest must be accepted and recited.

V. **Explanation:**

A. *Prayer to God for light and help* is important because only through God's grace can we hope to see sin as He sees it and to feel that supernatural sorrow that is necessary for the forgiveness of sins.

B. *An honest examination of conscience* is essential.

   1. A well-made confession begins, "Bless me, father, for I have sinned. It is two weeks (or whatever the correct time) since my last worthy confession." This statement of the lapse of time is important because

     a) The priest can then judge whether the penitent goes frequently or infrequently to confession.

     b) He can judge from the number of sins committed whether during a given time sin or a certain sin has become a habit.

     Thus two sins of thought over a period of six months indicates a very different state of soul from two sins of thought in one day.

     c) He may be sure whether or not the Easter duty has been performed.

C. *All mortal sins* must be confessed and their number given as exactly as possible.

   1. For **a mortal sin** three things are necessary:

     a) *Serious matter.*

     b) *Sufficient knowledge* of what one is doing at the time one is doing it.

     c) *Full consent of the will* to the act.

D. Serious matter:

   1. Often there is *no doubt* about this; one knows instinctively, from instruction, or in some other way that a thing is seriously wrong; e.g., a large theft; a deliberate sin of impurity.

   2. Sometimes there *is doubt* whether a certain thing is serious or not. In this case the confessor must be asked:

     a) "Father, is it a serious sin to steal $10?"

     b) In case one does not know the terms or words in which even to ask a question, one may say: "I have a question to ask about a matter that I do not know how to explain or express. Father, will you please help me?" The priest will gladly ask the necessary questions.

Note: It is a terrible mistake to fail to ask about sins when one has a doubt:

   a) If they are sins, the silence may mean that one has really concealed a serious sin.

   b) If they are not sins, much unhappiness can be avoided.

A troubled conscience in either case is avoided by a question asked the confessor.

    E. To discover one's sins one may think back over:

        1. The sin that causes most trouble and to which one is most frequently tempted.

        2. The sins by which one is likely to sin:

          a) Through mind.

          b) Through speech.

          c) Through eyes.

          d) Through ears.

          e) Through conduct.

        3. The sins that:

          a) Injure God.

          b) Do harm to friends and associates.

          c) Harm oneself.

          d) Cause unhappiness at home.

        4. The sins that mean the neglect of opportunities.

    F. *Sufficient knowledge.*

        1. This knowledge *must precede the act.*

          a) A person must know before he does a thing that it is wrong. If later on he finds out that the act was wrong, it was not a sin (unless he deliberately avoided knowing).

          b) He must be fully conscious at the time, i.e., before and during the acts, of what he is doing.

          Hence, things which occur in sleep, in semiconsciousness, in dreams, or when under the influence of ether, are not normally sins.

Note: If a person deliberately avoids knowing whether a thing is wrong, e.g., if he has a well-grounded doubt, does not inquire, but goes ahead and while in doubt takes a chance, this is culpable ignorance, and he is responsible for the sin.

    G. *Full consent.*

        1. The person, knowing that this is a sin, must want it and deliberately choose it.

        2. Hence:

          a) *One cannot be physically forced* to commit a sin.

          b) If one is in a situation from which *he cannot escape,* he is not responsible for the events that occur in that situation unless he deliberately consents.

c) If one is not sure that he has consented, he has not consented. If he has any doubt about consent, there is no doubt about it; because if he doubts his consent, he did not fully consent.

d) Violence eliminates free consent.

Scrupulous people are those who worry because they cannot be sure whether or not they consented.

Rules: 1. Since they are not sure, they did not fully consent. Hence, there is no sin there.

2. They must to secure peace of mind take the word of their confessor who, though they may not understand this, knows them better than they know themselves.

3. They must examine their consciences very briefly.

H. All mortal sins must be confessed and their number given, at least approximately.

I. Venial sins:

1. Need never be confessed.

2. Some of them should be confessed if there is no serious sin.

3. It is well but not necessary to give exact numbers.

4. It is well to tell some of them, especially when they are the cause of annoyance or trouble to others or may lead one into habits of sin.

5. Sins confessed are more likely to be forgiven since toward them the contrition is directed.

J. *Real, sincere, and supernatural sorrow for sins.*

Without sorrow for sin, confession is valueless.

a) Sorrow for sin includes the following elements:

(1) *Regret* that one has ever committed the sin.

(2) Because of some *supernatural consequences* for sin.

(3) And a determination with God's help not to commit serious sin again. If venial sins are confessed, one must be determined to avoid them also.

If any of these three elements is lacking, the confession is worthless and the sins remain unforgiven.

(4) *Regret* that one has committed the sin implies the realization that sin is a terrible evil, has offended God, and should not have been done.

b) *The supernatural reasons* for the sorrow are:

(1) *Imperfect,* and based on some supernatural consequence to the person sinning:

(*a*) The sinner will be punished forever in the *pains of hell*.

(*b*) The sinner will never have the *happiness of heaven*.

(2) *Perfect*, and based on the consequences of the sin to God who was offended by it.

(*a*) Mortal sin *crucified Jesus Christ*, and therefore the sinner hates the sin because it killed the Merciful Savior.

(*b*) Mortal sin is a crime against God who is the best of fathers, infinitely good in Himself and infinitely worthy of all our love, while sin does its best to spoil His kingdom and His hopes for the world.

With confession, imperfect contrition is enough. Without confession, perfect contrition is necessary. But it is well to try to have perfect contrition because:

a) More of the temporal punishment due mortal sin even when forgiven is remitted.

b) More venial sins are forgiven.

c) If some time one were in a position that demanded perfect contrition, e.g., an accident without help near from a priest, the practice of perfect contrition would make sorrow more easy.

K. Firm determination not to sin again means:

1. With the help of God's grace, the sinner means to avoid that sin.

2. As well as the conditions under which that sin will easily be committed.

He may realize that he is weak and likely to be severely tempted. But here and now he realizes that sin is evil, does him vast harm, and that he can with the help of God avoid it. This he means to do even when from experience he knows his own weakness.

L. An honest recital of the sins to the priest.

1. Clearly, simply, without exaggeration or minimizing, the penitent must tell his sins, making it sufficiently clear for the priest to understand, and answering the questions which the priest may need to ask.

VI. **The purposes of Confession** are:

A. *To receive forgiveness for our sins*, serious and venial, through the words of absolution.

B. *To free the soul from the punishments* due sin in hell, in purgatory, and on earth.

C. *To obtain the grace of the sacrament,* that is, strength to avoid these same sins or similar sins for the future and strength against all temptation.

D. *To receive from the priest such advice and guidance* as will help one to a life more according to the ideals of Christ.

VII. **Advice and Guidance:**

A. In the confessional the priest sits not merely as the judge and the dispenser of God's mercy, but *as the physician and guide* of souls. Hence, the penitent should feel free:

1. *To ask advice* about himself.
   a) How better to fight against evil and against temptation.
   b) How better to advance in strength and virtue.
   c) What course to pursue:
   (1) In immediate difficulties.
   (2) In choosing a state of life.
   (3) In problems that need solution.

VIII. *The Penance* is given as a punishment for the sin committed.
   By it the penitent:

A. Proves his sorrow.

B. Satisfies the justice of God for the crime committed.

C. Removes punishment due in purgatory.

D. So that it may not be forgotten, the penance should be said immediately following the confession.

IX. The practice of making good and frequent confessions begun during college days will be an invaluable aid to the good life the student hopes to live later on.

Note: Sometimes penitents find it easier to consult the priest outside of confession, and follow this consultation with confession.

Problems and Discussions

1. What is the parallel between the accusation of the Jews against Christ regarding the forgiveness of sins and the accusations of the non-Catholic against the priest?
2. Does the priest forgive sins? Or does Jesus Christ alone forgive them?
3. What could be said to change the attitude of a person who remarked: "I'm going to confession, and I certainly hate and dread it"?

4. Would you prefer a prayer for light that you said from your heart to one that you got from the prayer book?

5. Discuss this statement of a young person: "It's Friday night, and I'm going to confession tomorrow. So here's where I cut loose."

6. A friend steals $10 from you. He tells you he is sorry. On the way out he steals another $10 from you. What would you argue about his profession of sorrow? Compare him with the person who tells God he is sorry and then immediately sins once more.

7. Discuss these cases:

   a) A person steals $25. He is not sure later on whether this is a venial or mortal sin, so he decides as he does not know, he'll not say anything about it in confession.

   b) A person confesses: "I was immodest in thought once," because he is ashamed to admit that it was three times.

   c) Because he does not know how to explain a certain sin or by what name to call it, a penitent says nothing about it in confession.

   d) A person is in such a rush to get to a football game that he fails to examine his conscience and omits a serious sin.

   e) While half asleep, R finds evil thoughts have been going through his head, and he does not know whether to confess them or not.

   f) An improper picture is in a window. S sees it as he passes by, looks at it without fully realizing it is evil and later wonders if his glance was sinful.

   g) T gets himself (or herself) partly drunk knowing that under these circumstances he (or she) will more easily and without full consciousness do something that is wrong.

   h) V has heard vaguely that telling dirty stories is wrong. Deliberately he does not find out for certain so that he will be ignorant of the law and not obliged to stop telling them.

8. Discuss the following types of contrition:

   a) A is sorry because he is going to jail for his sin.

   b) B is sorry because sins of the flesh scourged Jesus Christ.

   c) C is sorry because he broke his mother's heart.

   d) D is sorry because sin has hurt his health.

   e) E is sorry; if there were no hell, he thinks he probably would sin again; but as there is a hell, he won't sin again.

   f) F made a fool of himself and wishes he hadn't.

   g) G has stolen $35. He thinks this a pretty poor price to pay for the loss of heaven, but he has no intention of returning the money.

   h) H has committed impurity with K. In confession H tells the sin and expresses sorrow, but expects to go out with K after Communion and sin again.

9. Discuss the statement: "I have no serious sins to confess, so I don't bother to go to confession."

10. Discuss the statement: "I want the priest to give me absolution and let me go. I don't want him discussing things with me."

Note: 1. When one is not conscious of sin, even slight sin, it is well to go to confession for the graces received in confession, to tell some fault of which one is conscious, to mention a sin of the past life, and receive absolution for the sake of the grace and strength.

2. Penances are not always given in proportion to the sins confessed. They will depend frequently upon the priest, many of whom give light penances and themselves offer up prayers or good works in reparation for the sins of their penitents.

3. A good Catholic will go to confession about once in two weeks.

Suggested Readings

PAMPHLETS

The Queen's Work Press:
Fashionable Sin, Lord, S.J.
Prodigals and Christ, Lord, S.J.
Confession is a Joy? Lord, S.J.
The Paulist Press:
Confession of Sins a Divine Institution, Conway, C.S.P.
The Catholic Truth Society:
Why Catholics Go to Confession, Anstrucker.

BOOKS

Geddes, *The Catholic Church and Confession* (Calvert Series) (Macmillan).
Pallen, *As Man to Man* (Macmillan).
Sempel, *Heaven Open to Souls* (Benziger).
See the *Catholic Encyclopedia:* "The Sacrament of Penance"; "Confession"; "Contrition"; *et passim.*

Chapter XXV

PRIESTLY CONSULTATION

I. **The Priest** in the Catholic Church occupies a unique position:
  A. He is the *representative of Jesus Christ:*
    1. *Offering the Sacrifice of the Mass.*
    2. *Forgiving sins.*
    3. *Acting as dispenser of the sacraments.*
    4. *Preaching and teaching:*
      a) Not his own personal opinions and ideas; but
      b) The official message given to the world by Christ, and passed on and repeated by the priest.
  B. *He is the servant of the people.*

Note: The Pope calls himself officially *Servus Servorum Dei,* the servant of the servants of God.

    1. As servant or steward:
      a) He is *deeply concerned* with their salvation.
      b) He *ministers to them* through the sacraments.
      c) He is the *father of his people,* particularly of the poor, the young, and the sorrowful.
      d) He is the *official teacher of the flock,* and, next to the parents, the official teacher especially of the children.
  C. For all these purposes he is:
    1. *Trained* in a very special manner:
      a) To understand *the needs of souls.*
      b) To understand *the problems of sinners and of saints,* and of just ordinary people.
      c) To guide t*he aspirations of the good.*
      d) To act as:
        (1) *Father* of his people.
        (2) *Physician* of souls.
        (3) *Shepherd* of his flock.
        (4) *Spiritual lawyer* sitting in dispassionate judgment on the crimes of the people against God.
    2. *He gives up the right to any family* of his own, so that he can be the father of all his people.

a) *He does not marry,* so that no other love or interest can come between him and the love and care of souls.

b) *He is forbidden to take part in other businesses* so that his whole time is devoted to his Father's business, which is souls and their needs.

Note: In his **study for the priesthood,** he studies

1. *Moral theology* which is a comprehensive treatment based on God's law, the Church's legislation, and human experience, of the judgment and cure of sin and the development of virtues

2. *Pastoral theology,* which treats of the practical problems of individuals, human relationships, family difficulties, and the various cases that a priest will meet or may meet in his parish.

Hence, even a young priest comes splendidly trained for his work. Rapidly he acquires a *vast practical experience* to supplant this theoretical knowledge:

1. From his association with people.
2. From regular priestly consultations and conferences.
3. From the confessional with its varied types of people.

II. Hence, to **the educated Catholic the priest** is:

A. *Not merely the one who offers sacrifice* and administers the sacraments, important as this is, but also:

B. The interested *guide of souls.*

C. The *experienced consultant* in problems that are:
1. Purely spiritual.
2. Social, i.e., problems of family, of business ethics, of prospective marriage, etc.

D. *A father* eager to help his people; *a wise friend* who has been trained by education and experience and consecrated by his profession to intelligent and sympathetic dealing with individuals and their problems. This in proper measure is true of the **Religious Brothers and Sisters** who share with the priest:
1. The *teaching* function of the Church.
2. The *zeal* for souls.
3. The *training and experience* that fits them to deal with problems and aspirations.

Matters proper to confession, however, should as a rule be discussed in the confessional.

III. In a Catholic college **the student lives and studies** under the direction of the priests or Religious. Wisely, then, during these college days:

A. He avails himself of their direction and help.

B. He thus trains himself to seek the guidance and advice and assistance of priests in later years.

C. **Problems** that should be and easily can be referred to the priest or Religious for guidance are:

  1. All problems *connected with studies*. The Religious or priestly teacher is interested in his students' success in studies, knowing that often this means success in later life.

  2. The decision regarding *the choice of a career*. Usually one is guided best in choosing a career by the advice of someone who:

    a) Knows a person's abilities.

    b) Can judge his qualifications objectively.

    c) Can by his interest lead a person through discussion to a fuller realization of his own limitations, abilities, inclinations.

Note: Priests and Religious teachers do not "rope people" into priestly or Religious vocations. They know:

1. That a person without vocation would be unhappy in the life.

2. That they are often positively forbidden by their rule even to seem to persuade people to choose one rather than another vocation.

3. That practically some people are fitted by nature for one vocation, and others for quite another.

  3. *Doubts and difficulties against faith:*

    a) These often disappear when, instead of brooding over them, the student simply states them to some experienced person.

    b) Usually he learns that "doubt is a disease of youth and inexperience."

    c) Often the answer is simple and easy and satisfactory and ends an unnecessary amount of mental worry.

    d) More than likely, the one consulted has met this difficulty frequently before and knows just how to solve it.

    e) Consultation may mean the difference between peace of mind and real mental misery.

  4. *Moral problems.* (These, as a rule, should be discussed with a priest.)

a) These will always get a sympathetic hearing from the one consulted.

b) There is no such thing as a new problem. The individual will find that his problem is like that of thousands of others.

c) The consultant is "shockproof," trained by education and experience to face problems without embarrassment.

d) Many problems disappear as soon as they are put into words.

e) The heavy weight of a problem borne alone disappears when the problem is shared with someone else.

f) The consultant usually knows both the natural and supernatural remedies by which the problem can be solved.

g) The later and, if desired, continued interest in the person will solve future difficulties and problems.

5. *Family problems.* While many problems of family finance and family misunderstanding cannot be handled effectively by anyone but a member of the family, many others can wisely and profitably be referred to the priest or Religious:

a) To determine the correct course for the student himself to follow in its regard.

b) To find out the best advice to give those of the family who need it.

6. *Guidance in reading.* A young man or woman can learn from an experienced educator quite independently of class;

a) The worth-while books to read.

b) The books that are a waste of time or a danger to faith and morals.

IV. **The priest** can be consulted:

A. In the confessional after the telling of one's sins or without the necessity for telling one's sins, or before confession.

V. **The priest or Religious teacher** can be consulted:

A. In the classroom following (but not before) class lectures or recitations.

B. Frequently in their offices if they have them.

C. Sometimes (depending upon local customs and rules) in their rooms.

VI. This priestly and religious consultation should be regarded not as something unusual and exceptional, but as a wise habit to be contracted for use in later life. The priest will not interfere nor force his guidance and direction. But he will willingly and happily give the benefit of his training, education, and experience to those who need it and seek it.

Problems and Discussions

1. In what elements does the office of the priest differ essentially and clearly from that of a minister?
2. What would you say to the statement sometimes heard: "The priest is all right as long as he stays inside the altar rail"?
3. In what sense is the priest the shepherd and in what sense is he the servant of his flock?
4. In view of this discussion, explain the priest's favorite title, Father.
5. Discuss the frequent statement of young people: "I can run my own life without help from anyone."
6. Why should the fact that the priest is without wife or family give a person additional trust in him?
7. Since the Religious Brother or Sister shares the teaching office of the priest and his care for souls, why inevitably and in due measure, do they share his work as adviser and consultant?
8. Explain to a non-Catholic why the Catholic priest because of education and training and experience is not easily shocked.
9. List the various offices the priest holds in relation to the faithful.
10. What would you be justified to surmise of the young man or woman who at the close of a year in a Catholic college brags: "I went through the whole year without even speaking to a priest (or Religious) except during class hours"?
11. Discuss the following cases:
    a) A student entering junior class, because he does not particularly like Science, decides to take no more of it, and does so without consultation with his professor.
    b) A student goes through four years of college without any definite career in life ahead, but never asks the advice of anyone on what he seems best fitted to do.
    c) A student who feels perhaps he may have a priestly (or religious) vocation, never mentions it to anyone because he (or she) is afraid of being bothered or "roped in."
    d) A college student reads a book which seems to prove that the Gospels are not true history. He spends hours in the public library looking through books in the hope of answering the difficulties, but does it unadvised.

12. List some types of moral problems that could well be referred to a priest or Religious for advice.
13. What is meant by the seal of confession? How far is a priest or Religious bound to keep confidences given outside the confessional?
14. Discuss this statement: The student who during college days fails to find a good friend and adviser on the faculty, has missed a most important element in a Catholic college training.
15. Do you find this statement true: The busier the professor and the more people consulting him or her, the more time he or she seems to have for each individual?

Suggested Readings

PAMPHLETS

The Queen's Work Press:
My Friend the Pastor, Lord, S.J.

Chapter XXVI

PRAYER

I. **For the unbeliever,** *life is fixed and unchangeable,* cast in a mold that cannot be modified or broken.

    A. No God exists, or if He does, He cannot interfere in the affairs of men.

    B. Heredity and environment mold the life in what is a modern equivalent of fate.

II. **To the Catholic,** *life is shaped and determined:*

    A. By the fact that man has a *free will,* which makes it possible for him to pick and choose much of his way through life.

    B. By the *interest which God takes in him* and his destiny.

    C. By the *power of prayer* which man can freely use to win from an interested God the things he needs for life and its emergencies.

    D. Hence, to the Catholic the world is:

        1. Not a despotism ruled by a tyrant called Fate.

        2. But a monarchy in which a paternal Monarch accepts the petitions of His subjects and acts upon them.

    E. The Catholic, therefore, regards **prayer** *as his petition to a fatherly and powerful King,* who grants freely the favors asked.

III. **Prayer** is:

    A. *Conversation with God.*

        1. It is the friendly interview between a child and his sympathetic and powerful Father.

    B. *The humble but hopeful petition* of a subject to a gracious King.

    C. *The praise* and honor and gratitude shown to a Benefactor by the one benefited.

    D. *Sorrow* expressed for the wrongs done an offended Benefactor or Father or King.

    E. *The thoughtful consideration* of God's relations with His world, as Creator, Redeemer, Sanctifier.

    F. *The request to a saint* to pray to God more effectively than we can ever hope to pray.

IV. Prayer is necessary:

A. *Christ spent much of His life* instructing men in the need of prayer and in the manner in which prayer could be made. He gave the example of almost ceaseless prayer, beginning all His important actions with prayer, and coupling work with prayer in an uninterrupted union.

B. We ourselves know:

1. *We have offended God.* Hence, we must ask His forgiveness.

2. *We are deep in God's debt* for the blessings He has given us. Hence, we must thank Him.

3. *We are surrounded by pressing needs* that only God can supply.

4. *We are His children;* hence, we must express our love: His subjects; hence we must express our loyal homage.

V. The power of prayer was expressed by Christ in this magnificent promise: *"Whatsoever you shall ask the Father in My name,* He will give it to you. Ask and you shall receive."

A. Hence, *Christ guarantees infallibly* that prayer will be answered:

1. If we ask with *faith* in Christ's promise.

2. If we ask with an *insistence* that proves our sincerity.

3. If the thing we ask is *for our good.*

Note: If it is not for our good, God, who sees the future that we cannot know, will not give it to us. He would be cruel if He gave us what He knows will hurt us. But no prayer is wasted. So when the things we ask are not given to us because they are bad for us, God answers our prayer by giving us something that will be for our good.

VI. Christ gave us the perfect prayer, and to show us how simple prayer is, He showed us:

A. That the wording of prayer should be absolutely *natural* and from our hearts.

It is not necessary to be clever, to talk to God in oratory or poetry. God wants our simple, natural speech.

B. That in prayer we must remember *God's interests,* the interests of the world, as well as our own concerns and needs.

C. That when we pray we can come as *confident children,* who address:

1. *"Our Father":* At once we establish the beautiful relationship of children and their father.

2. *"Who art in heaven"*: We turn from the affairs of earth to consider the important affairs of eternity.

3. *"Hallowed be Thy name"*: We pray that God's creatures will bless and serve Him as His power and goodness deserve.

4. *"Thy Kingdom come"*: If it does, it means happiness for all mankind, and glory for God.

5. *"Thy will be done"*: In the fulfillment of that will, creation will achieve its highest purpose; men their highest peace, happiness, and destiny.

6. *"On earth as it is in heaven"*: The angels find their joy in doing in heaven what men do so reluctantly on earth.

7. *"Give us this day our daily bread"*: We lay before God the needs of our bodies.

8. *"And forgive us our trespasses"*: We admit we are sinners, and beg Him to wash those sins from our souls.

9. *"As we forgive those who trespass against us"*: We, in turn, forgive those who have wronged us, proving to God we deserve His forgiveness.

10. *"And lead us not into temptation"*: We will walk safely through the dangers of life, if God protects us and keeps us safe.

11. *"But deliver us from evil"*: God alone can protect us from all possible harm to soul and body. We beg this, knowing that He is eager so to do.

VII. Through prayer:

A. We become *like the angels,* talking to God, praising Him.

B. We grow *strong* in the grace He gives us in answer to prayer.

C. *Earth seems less important* and heaven more so.

D. We gain *graces and blessings* for our daily lives.

E. We *supernaturalize* our actions.

F. We influence the *course of history* for good, winning God's favor for rulers, needy, sick, poor, young, endangered, etc.

G. We *repay the benefits* we have received from others by commending them to God in prayer.

VIII. Vocal Prayer is the type best known. It is the use of definite words by which we address God.

A. The college student's day will rightly begin with the *Morning Offering,* by which he consecrates every moment and every act of the day and makes it meritorious with God.

B. *Each class* is usually preceded by and followed by prayer;

in this way the study, lecture, laboratory is dedicated to God
and merits grace for the student and others.

C. *In the morning,* the college student will make his acts of
faith, hope, and charity, commend himself to Mary, his
guardian angel, his patron saint, and ask the Savior the
grace to live in His footsteps.

D. *In the evening,* he will make an *examination of conscience*
based on the one he has learned to make for confession. He
will thank God for the blessings of the day, and commend
his safety during the night to Christ, Mary, the saints, and
his guardian angel.

E. *Vocal prayer* will for him include the use of:

1. The magnificent prayers of the *Liturgy of the Church:*
The Mass prayers, the psalms, the official prayers of the
Church.

2. The use of his *rosary:* Every student will carry his rosary
always with him.

3. The occasional use of the *Litany of the Blessed Virgin,*
the Holy Name, the Blessed Sacrament, some favorite
saint.

4. The magnificent prayers like the *Angelus,* the prayers
following Holy Communion, etc.

IX. **Mental Prayer,** however, is typical of the intelligent college student. It is the thoughtful consideration of the truths of faith, the
events in the life of our Lord and His saints, with resolutions
drawn from these considerations and applied to the student's
own life.

A. The following **methods** are suggested:

1. *Phrase by phrase,* slowly and thoughtfully, a favorite prayer
is recited. The student pauses on each phrase long enough to
consider fully its meaning and apply that meaning to himself.
Hail — Mary — full of grace — the Lord — is with thee — etc.

2. *In the presence of the Blessed Sacrament,* he recalls who is
present, why He is present, with what love, in what loneliness,
at what cost to Himself, with what blessings for the worshiper,
and with what sort of return from the faithful, especially the
student himself.

3. Using the *beads to measure* the length of his thought, he
says the Rosary, thinking carefully and vividly on each event
as it is indicated in the individual mysteries.

4. He makes the *Stations of the Cross,* looking at the pictures,

studying the actions, thoughts, sufferings of Christ, realizing why He does all this, thinking then of his own sins and their effect upon the suffering Christ.

5. Slowly and deliberately he reads *a short scene from the Gospel,* tries to visualize just what occurred, to see and hear what Christ says and does, to imagine himself among the crowd or the Apostles or the worshipers, and then determines to live as Christ is teaching him to live.

6. He thinks quietly upon *the great truths of religion:* eternity, heaven, hell, the certainty of death, the beauty of faith, the effects of sin, the delight of virtue.

B. **This type of prayer** is most important for the student:

1. It is of an *intellectual character* that suits his needs.

2. It *trains the mind* to think naturally of God and spiritual things.

3. It makes *religion sink deep* into the soul.

4. It leads to *correct conduct,* for one who thinks correctly will act correctly.

5. It proves to the student that *formal words and expressions,* the fixed prayers and phrases of the prayer book are *not necessary* for a high type of prayer.

X. *Prayer must unselfishly* include the needs and necessities of others. One can safely ask for oneself, but one should never rest content with merely prayer for oneself.

A. In praying for oneself, one should start with *the needs of one's soul:*

1. Strength against temptation.

2. Faith, firm and vigorous.

3. An increase of grace.

4. A deeper knowledge and love of our Savior.

5. Real sorrow for sin.

B. Then the *needs of the mind* should be presented:

1. Success in studies.

2. Success in one's vocation later on.

3. The grace to know what God wishes one to do.

C. Finally the *needs of one's body.*

1. Health.

2. The necessities of life.

3. Such comforts as will help one on one's way through life.

D. One should then remember the *needs of others:*
1. One's own relatives.
2. Classmates and friends.
3. Those one has offended and harmed.
4. The Church with its priests and Religious.
5. Rulers: The Pope, bishops, the President.
6. Those laboring for souls, that their work may be blessed.
7. Sinners, especially those in danger of death.
8. Young people throughout the world.
9. Those who are severely tempted.
10. Those who do not possess the faith.
E. Great causes: Peace, freedom from persecution, etc.

XI. **Prayer** may be addressed directly:
A. *To God, the Father.*
B. *To God, the Son,* especially after Holy Communion and before the tabernacle.
C. *To the Holy Ghost.*
1. The bodies of those who are baptized and especially those who have received confirmation are the temples of the Holy Ghost. The student, then, can turn his thoughts inward and talk directly to the Spirit of Wisdom and Strength and Love who is physically present in his heart.

XII. Prayer may be addressed to:
A. *Our Mother,* who is our powerful intercessor.
B. *Our patron saints,* who are interested in us and much in the favor of God.
C. *The souls in purgatory,* needing our help, yet able to help us.
D. *To our Guardian Angels,* who see the face of our Father, and carry our message direct to him.

XIII. Prayers may be *very short,* that is, ejaculations: The quick cry to God in temptation, sudden need, sorrow, gratitude, realization of His presence.

Note: A habit of prayer developed during college days will be the strongest source of courage and grace later on.

Problems and Discussions

1. Discuss this statement: "I am willing to work for God; but I can't waste time and energy praying."

2. Show from Christ's life that He really did set us the example of prayer.
3. Why is a Christian who believes in prayer far freer than a pagan who says that prayer is unavailing?
4. Which type of prayer most appeals to you?
5. To many Protestants, prayer is simply an emotional release by which "I let off spiritual steam." Is this a true idea of prayer?
6. Prove to a fellow student that prayer is necessary for the average college man or woman.
7. A young man or woman says: "I prayed to be elected president of my class. I wasn't. So I have ceased praying. I no longer believe in the power of prayer." Discuss this with him.
8. A student prays for a chance to get even with an enemy. What would God's attitude be toward such a prayer?
9. A student feels that he has fulfilled his obligation of prayer when he asks God for the things he wants. Do you agree?
10. Show that the Act of Contrition, phrase by phrase, is a satisfactory prayer.
11. The pagan says: "A man down on his knees is debased and humiliated." The Catholic says: "A man on his knees in prayer is ennobled and dignified and splendidly human." Which is right, and why?
12. What vocal prayers do you consider that a student should say every day? Which at least several times a month?
13. If it is true that "With desolation is the whole world made desolate because there is no man that thinketh in his heart," would mental prayer be the answer to this peril?
14. Show a friend that mental prayer is really not difficult.
15. Discuss the following cases:
    a) A prays for a new fur coat.
    b) B prays for a good husband.
    c) C prays that God will give him just the things that will be best for him.
    d) D prays: "God, give me grace to overcome temptations."
    e) E prays for grace for missionaries.
    f) F prays: "God, give grace and strength to Your priests."
    g) G prays: "Please take care of my parents."
    h) H prays: "Make me popular at the Prom."
    i) I prays: "Bring me through the week-end without sin."
    j) J prays: "Be merciful to some sinner dying tonight."

Suggested Readings

PAMPHLETS

The Paulist Press:
The Our Father, Grau, S.J.
Praying to Saints, Smith, S.J.

Prayer, Elliot, C.S.P.
The Catholic Truth Society:
   How to Converse with God, Boutauld.
   How to Make Mental Prayer, Chenart.

BOOKLETS

LeBuffe, *"Let Us Pray" Series* (America Press).
LeBuffe, *"As It is Written" Series* (America Press).
See the *Catholic Encyclopedia:* "Prayer."

Chapter XXVII

CATHOLIC ACTION

I. **Religion is not a mere theory.** It involves a set of principles that must be **put at once into practice.**

II. Nor is religion something to be merely thought about, approved, intellectually weighed, but left without effect upon oneself or others.

III. Least of all is religion to be confined to Sunday mornings and to night and morning prayers. It must be the *dominant factor in the conduct of everyday life.* For:
    A. Religion embraces a complete theory of life:
        1. That dominates one's work, one's study, one's social activities, one's amusements, one's relations with God, country, home, and fellow men in all their aspects.
    B. To many a non-Catholic religion is merely a correct but largely ineffective social convention, a pleasant emotional release. To the Catholic it is *the element in life that determines all other elements* since:
        1. It gives the reason for life.
        2. It points out the objectives of life.
        3. It teaches the correct way to live that life.
        4. It indicates the essential relationships of life.
        5. It places the essential foundations for morality.
    C. Hence, a *thorough Catholic* who understands the importance of his religion and its complete solution of life is a Catholic:
        1. When *working* at his profession or business.
        2. In his loyalty *to the state.*
        3. In his dealings with his *fellow men.*
        4. In his choice of recreation and *amusement.*
        5. In his thought, *attitude toward life* and its values, conversation, reading, etc.
        6. This does not mean that he thrusts his religion into the faces of others. It does mean, however:
           a) That never does he do or take part in or say or approve

things that give the lie to his faith. He cannot as a Catholic be a party to:

(1) Dishonest business.

(2) Crooked politics.

(3) Immoral forms of entertainment.

(4) Injustice or cruelty toward anyone.

(5) Movements that are condemned by nature or the Church.

(6) Forms of literature or art that are pagan and anti Christian.

b) That he honestly tries *to bring to his everyday life and his dealings with others* and with all the world:

(1) *The principles of Jesus Christ.*

(2) *As explained by the Catholic Church,* which applies these principles to modern problems.

Note: This application is found:

1. In the **Pope's Encyclicals,** notably those dealing with Marriage, the State, Education, Capital and Labor, Charity, Business, Communism, etc.

2. In the growing volume of **Catholic Literature,** produced to meet modern needs and answer modern questions.

IV. A really educated Catholic:

A. Knows the *theory of religion:*

1. *From his religion class,* in which he intelligently, logically, and systematically has the Catholic viewpoint on life explained to him.

2. *From his philosophy class,* in which the great questions of life are discussed and analyzed, and their answers presented and proved.

3. *From the whole trend of his Catholic college training:* In science, literature, history, and economics, seen with a fair presentation of anti- or un-Catholic arguments and attitudes, but an insistence on the positive Catholic side.

4. From his intelligent and growing *acquaintance with Catholic literature.*

Note: The volume of **Catholic Literature** grows continuously in size, intrinsic worth, and interested acceptance by Catholics and non-Catholics. The educated Catholic will know this field thoroughly:

1. For his own information and mental assurance and satisfaction.

2. As something about which he will be asked and to which he must refer the non-Catholic thinker.

    B. Has learned *to apply this theory to life.*

       1. He is not content with abstract religion, but uses it immediately and effectively:

         a) For himself.

         b) For others.

Note: 1. No one ever really learns anything which someone else merely explains to him.

Hence, the surprising ignorance of people who merely listen to lectures, and the astonishing ignorance of classes when the teacher lectures and does all the work.

2. One knows best the thing which one finds personally interesting. Hence the need of mental alertness, interest, and mental response if one is to learn.

    3. One fully clinches knowledge when:

       a) One teaches what one knows to others:

         (1) Either by formal teaching.

         (2) By intelligent discussion or conversation.

         (3) By writing upon the subject with others in view.

       b) One puts into practice what one has learned, e.g.: Through the physics laboratory of the physics course. In piano practice to supplement musical theory. Thus: in religion one learns:

         Holy Communion is important; therefore one must and does go frequently.

         Mass is our sacrifice; therefore we learn to offer it and do offer it with the priest.

         Charity is the greatest of the virtues; therefore one actually practices charity to the poor, sick, blind, young.

         The Catholic truth is the hope and salvation of mankind; therefore one helps spread that truth by mission support, the distribution of Catholic literature, lectures, the teaching of catechism, etc.

         The written word is powerful for truth or error; therefore one learns to write and actually does write on Catholic subjects.

         Effective organization and planning is necessary for the advancement of the Catholic cause; therefore one learns to organize and plan while at college.

         All Catholics are brothers and sisters; therefore one drops

the terrible suspicion and dislike found sometimes between Catholic schools and unites in projects like the Sodality of Our Lady and the Catholic Students' Mission Crusade, which bring students together in union and charity.

V. All this is the underlying idea of the **Holy Father** who is calling Catholics to **Catholic Action**:

    A. He does *not* wish them to be *unintelligent,* sheeplike Catholics.

    B. *Uninterested and unconcerned* about Catholic truth and the mission of our Savior and His Church to the world.

    C. But mentally *alert, intelligent, apostolic,* knowing their faith and loving it and realizing its value to the world.

    D. Who *live it* in every detail of their lives.

    E. Thus presenting it effectively as *an exemplified theory* of life to the non-Catholic world.

VI. **Catholic Action,** *then, is religion carried into every detail of life.*

    A. *It is the active participation of the laity in the apostolic mission of the hierarchy.*

    B. Thus:

        1. It is *religion dominating* life.

        2. The *layman shares the work* of the bishops and priests who are consecrated and ordained to bring Jesus Christ to the world that needs Him.

        3. The priest's whole life is supposed *to be a living out in action of his faith.* So the life of the active layman is supposed to be the living out in action of his faith.

VII. Hence, while at college, the **Catholic college student must determine**:

    A. *To master the theory of his faith,* not because it is a classroom subject but because it is a divinely inspired and reasonably proved synthesis of principles by which life is most effectively and successfully lived.

    B. *To learn to apply this theory to life* immediately, and while he or she is still a student, without waiting for a vague later day.

Note: In later life a man or woman will do only with difficulty what he has not learned to do easily and well at school.

Hence: 1. The college expects the student to regard *religion and philosophy classes* as the most important classes of his course.

    2. It offers its **Catholic Action Organization,** usually *the Sodality of Our Lady,* as the laboratory of religion class and the opportunity for the student to learn how Catholic Action can be:
    Lived
    Planned
    Talked
    Written
    Publicized
    Put into immediate effect
    Made to reach and influence others.

VIII. **The Sodality of Our Lady** has been the widely accepted Catholic Action organization for students because:

    A. It is an association *canonically erected* and approved by Rome, and *endowed with matchless blessings* and favors granted to its members by the Holy See.

    B. Since it exists *in the vast majority of Catholic colleges,* it unites the college students in a national and international spirit of Catholic unity.

    C. In its *three hundred and fifty years* it has enrolled among its members saints, popes, kings, distinguished statesmen and soldiers, the flower of intellectual manhood and womanhood.

    D. Under the *patronage of our heavenly Mother,* it presents as its first objective loyalty and devotion to Christ, especially in the Blessed Sacrament.

    E. It stresses *personal holiness,* the necessity of an exemplary life, offers mental and vocal prayer, loyalty to the person of Christ and love for Mary Immaculate.

    F. It has a highly *developed intellectual program of* writing, speaking, discussion, study, Catholic evidence, truth presentations, all appealing to the college mentality.

    G. It offers unexampled opportunity for *learning student leadership* in Catholic Action through its system of the Students' Spiritual Council and active committees.

    H. It turns the eyes of the student toward his *parish,* the logical and inevitable center of Catholic Action.

    I. It offers the widest *variety of activities* by which the principles of encyclicals may be applied by students to their immediate life.

    J. It has united the colleges of various localities in local *Col-*

lege Councils on Catholic Action, stimulating the activities of the individual colleges and uniting in common enterprises.

K. It has regular *national College Conventions* on Catholic Action and annual Summer Schools of Catholic Action to develop student leadership.

L. Its *Central Office* established in St. Louis willingly and freely services colleges that wish to expand and improve their Catholic Action program.

IX. Whatever the Catholic Action organization, it should be regarded by the student:

A. As the most important society of the school.

B. As his opportunity to apply the theory of religion and philosophy classes to life.

C. As his training school of future Catholic leadership.

X. As a result of his Catholic college training and its immediate exercise through the Sodality of Our Lady, **the student must expect to leave school:**

A. *With a loyalty to Christ* that shows itself in appreciation of the liturgy, frequent Communion, an intelligent attitude toward retreats, mental prayer.

B. *With a love of Mary* that shows itself in personal purity, correct social attitudes, and prayer to and trust in her.

C. *An intelligent grasp of the essentials of Catholic faith* and Scholastic Philosophy, and a ready ability to present these essentials to others.

D. Experience in *planning religious programs* and work.

E. An ability to *talk intelligently* on the Catholic solution of modern problems.

F. An ability to *teach the essentials* of faith to someone else.

G. If he can write at all, some real *experience in writing* on Catholic subjects.

H. Some experience in the *Apostolic life:* work for the missions, actual charitable work done while in college, some type of apostolic work undertaken successfully.

I. A fair knowledge of *Catholic literature* and how it can be effectively brought to the hands of others.

J. An ability *to work effectively with others,* those of his own college and those of other colleges.

K. A realization that no matter from what college a student

comes, they are *both Catholics* and hence united in spirit and objective.

L. A determination to carry the principles of the Pope's encyclicals into his professional, business, and social life.

XI. The Parish.

A. Correctly or incorrectly many college students are accused of lacking interest in their parish. They should, on the contrary, feel *a deep gratitude to their parish:*

1. Through it they receive the grace of the sacraments.
2. Through it they receive the benefit of the *Missa pro Populo.*
3. Through it they usually receive their Catholic education.

B. They must also feel a *deep responsibility to that parish:*

1. Belonging to at least *one parish organization,* and giving it the benefit of their trained experience.
2. Realizing that *Catholic Action* is first to be displayed *in coöperation with the parish clergy.*
3. Hence taking part in *whatever promotes the good of the parish.*
4. Setting the parish an *example of trained Catholic loyalty.*

Problems and Discussions

1. It has been said of some people that they put on and off their religion with their Sunday clothes. Discuss this attitude.
2. Explain the expression: "Catholic Action is twenty-four-hour-a-day religion."
3. Is it true that a man's or woman's religion is sometimes proved more clearly by what he does outside of Church than by what he does while in Church? Give instances.
4. Explain to a non-Catholic why a Catholic feels that religion must dominate the whole of life.
5. Describe the daily and personal conduct of a Catholic who is convinced he must always be a Catholic: What he omits; what he naturally tends to do; the type of his conversation; the way in which he performs his various actions, etc.
6. Of a Catholic business man it is said: "His word is as good as his bond." Show the relation of this conduct to Catholic Action.
7. Of a Catholic woman it is said: "When she entertains, her parties are clever, amusing, interesting, delightful; but she tolerates nothing vulgar, common, or sinful." Show the connection of this conduct and Catholic Action.

8. Give three or four definitions or descriptions of Catholic Action with examples illustrating each description.

9. Why does Catholic Action seem particularly suited to our age?

10. Discuss the following people from the angle of Catholic Action:

   a) A ushers in the church at the last Mass, but steals $200,000 from the city through a fraudulent paving contract.

   b) B sings soprano at the High Mass, but the young men of the neighborhood discuss her social conduct freely among themselves.

   c) C raised his employees' wages when he read what the Pope said about a living wage.

   d) D asked a young man to leave when he became intoxicated with drink he himself had brought at her party.

   e) E is a frequent communicant, but declines to contribute to the missions on the ground that "we have enough to do at home."

   f) F is a "good Catholic" whenever election time comes 'round and he needs the Catholic vote.

   g) G lives up to this principle: "The finest lesson I can preach to my non-Catholic business associates is the lesson of my absolute honesty."

   h) H is a Catholic mother who allows her children to bring any sort of literature into the house, and never notices what sort of movies they go to see.

   i) I, a college girl, out over a week-end, is much more hilarious and loose in her conduct than the non-Catholics present.

   j) J reads once a week to the old blind in a neighboring Old Peoples' Home.

11. What explanation can you give for the fact that after years of religious education so many people are ignorant of their faith? What would you suggest as remedies for this situation?

12. Explain the statement: A purely theoretical Catholic is a bad Catholic.

13. Analyze and discuss this statement made by a convention of college students: "For college men and women, Catholic Action fundamentally consists in leading lives of exemplary character, in developing an intellectual appreciation of their faith, and a willingness and ability to present that faith convincingly to others."

14. Prove from examples taken from various fields that one learns best the thing in which he is interested. That one clinches knowledge through teaching others. That only by putting theory into practice is theory finally mastered.

15. Illustrate this from the field of religion.

16. Describe what you feel would be an ideal college Catholic Action organization.

17. What should be the attitude of a student appreciative of his faith when he learns he has been asked by the Holy Father to coöperate in the work of the priesthood?
18. Could Catholic Action be fostered by individual professors in particular courses? Explain your answer.
19. Is there value in college students developing a society that unites them with the students of other colleges throughout the country and the world?
20. Discuss the Sodality of Our Lady as a Catholic Action organization.
21. Discuss the duty of a college student to his parish.
22. Describe a well-rounded Catholic college graduate.

Suggested Readings

The Papal Encyclicals on:
Retreats
Education
Christian Marriage
Labor
Reconstruction

PAMPHLETS:

The Queen's Work Press:
The Call to Catholic Action, Lord, S.J.

Reading List

My thanks are especially due to Mr. Calvert Alexander, S.J., and Sister Mary Genevieve of Notre Dame College, South Euclid, Ohio, for their extensive help and guidance in compiling the book lists.

Note: Students are expected to read a number of these books, depending on the direction of the instructor, as an essential supplement to the textbook.

Adam, Karl, *Christ and the Western Mind* (Sheed and Ward, 1933).
——— *Christ, Our Brother* (Sheed and Ward, 1931).
——— *The Spirit of Catholicism* (Macmillan, 1929).

Barry, Wm. F., *Cardinal Newman* (Scribner's, 1904).
Belloc, Hilaire, *A Companion to Mr. Well's Outline of History* (Sheed and Ward, 1926).
——— *Cranmer* (Lippincott, 1931).
——— *Essays of a Catholic* (Sheed and Ward, 1931).
——— *Europe and the Faith* (Paulist Press, 1921).
——— *The Free Press.*
——— *How the Reformation Happened* (McBride, 1928).
——— *Path to Rome* (Putnam, 1915).
——— *Survivals and New Arrivals* (Macmillan, 1929).
——— *Wolsey* (Lippincott, 1931).
Belloc, Bessie, Rainer, *Historic Nuns* (Duckworth, 1898).
Belloc, Knox, Goodier, Kaye-Smith, *Why I Am and Why I Am Not a Catholic* (Macmillan, 1930).
Benson, R. H., *None Other God* (Herder, 1911).
——— *Initiation* (Dodd, 1914).
——— *Religion of the Plain Man* (Benziger, 1906).
Blunt, H., *Great Wives and Mothers* (Devin-Adair, 1917).
Benedictines of Ramsgate, *Book of the Saints* (compilation). (London, A. & C. Black, 1921).
Brégy, Catherine, *Poets and Pilgrims* (Benziger, 1925).
——— *Poets' Chantry* (Herder, 1912).
Bridgett, T. E., *Our Lady's Dowry* (Burns and Oates, 1875).

Calvert Series (Macmillan).
Camm, Bede, *English Martyrs* (Longmans, 1932).
Chesterton, Mrs. A. E., *St. Teresa* (Doubleday, Doran, 1928).
Chesterton, G. K., *Catholic Church and Conversion* (Macmillan, 1926).
——— *Collected Poems,* cf., "Ballad of the White Horse" and "Lepanto" (Cecil Palmer, 1927).
——— *The Everlasting Man* (Dodd, 1925).

———— *Heretics* (Dodd, 1905).
———— *Orthodoxy* (Dodd, 1909).
———— *The Thing* (Dodd, 1930).
Claudel, Paul, *Letters to a Doubter* (Boni, 1927).
Connolly, Myles, *Mr. Blue* (Macmillan, 1928).
Conway, *The Question Box* (Paulist Press, new ed., 1929).
Cram, Ralph Adams, *The Catholic Church and Art* (Macmillan, 1930).
Curtayne, Alice, *St. Catherine of Siena* (Sheed and Ward, 1930).

D'Arcy, Martin, S.J., *The Life of the Church* (Dial Press, 1932).
Dawson, Christopher, *The Making of Europe* (Sheed and Ward, 1932).
———— *The Modern Dilemma* (Sheed and Ward, 1932).
Delany, S. P., *Why Rome* (N. Y., L. MacVeagh, the Dial Press; Toronto, Longmans, Green, 1930).
Driscoll, *Convert Literary Women* (Magnificat Press, 1928).
Dudley, *Shadow on the Earth* (Longmans, 1924).
———— *The Masterful Monk* (Longmans, 1929).
———— *The Pageant of Life* (Longmans, 1932).
———— *The English Way* (Sheed and Ward, 1933). (English Saints by Well-known Authors.)

Essays in Order No. 1 (Macmillan, 1931).
Essays in Order No. 2 (Sheed and Ward) (*Religion and Culture,* by Maritain, 1931; *Crisis in the West,* by Wust, 1931; *Christianity and the New Age,* by Dawson, 1931).
Eustace, C. J., *Romewards* (Benziger, 1932).

Fouard, *Last Years of St. Paul* (Longmans, 1900).
———— *St. John at the Close of the Apostolic Age* (Longmans, 1906).
———— *St. Paul and His Mission* (Longmans, 1894).
———— *St. Peter and the First Years of Christianity* (Longmans, 1892).
Fry, Penrose, *The Church Surprising* (Cassell, 1932).

Geddes, Leonard, S.J., *The Catholic Church and Confession* (Macmillan, 1928).
Gerard, John, *The Old Riddle and the Newest Answer* (Longmans, 1924 — 4th ed.).
Gheon, Henri, *Secret of the Cure d'Ars* (Sheed and Ward; Longmans, 1929).
Gillis, James M., C.S.P., *False Prophets* (Macmillan, 1925).
Goodier, Alban, *Inner Life of the Church* (Longmans, 1933).

Hollis, Christopher, *The Monstrous Regiment* (Sheed and Ward, 1929).
Horgan, John, *Great Catholic Laymen* (Dublin C.T.S., 1905).

———— *The Irish Way* (Sheed and Ward, 1932) (Short Lives of Saints from Patrick to Matt Talbot).

Johnson, Vernon, *One Lord, One Faith* (Sheed and Ward, 1929).

Kelly, B. W., *Some Great Catholics of Church and State.*
Klein, Felix, *Madeleine Semer, Convert and Mystic* (Macmillan, 1927).
Knox, Ronald, *Broadcast Minds* (Sheed and Ward, 1932).
———— *Essays in Satire* (Dutton, 1930).
———— *A Spiritual Æneid* (Longmans, 1918).
Kurth, G., *The Church at the Turning Points of History* (Naegele, 1918).

LaFarge, John, S.J., *Four Great Converts* (America Press: pamphlet).
LeBec, E., *A Medical Proof of the Miraculous* (Kenedy, 1923).
Lewis, D. B. Wyndham, *Charles of Europe* (Coward-McCann, 1931).
Lunn, Arnold, *The Flight from Reason* (The Dial Press, 1931).

May, J. Lewis, *Cardinal Newman* (MacVeagh, 1930).
Marshall, Bruce, *Father Malachy's Miracle* (Doubleday Doran, 1931).
Massis, Henri, *The Defense of the West* (Harcourt, 1928).
McNabb, Vincent, O.P., *The Catholic Church and Philosophy* (Macmillan, 1927).
Mercier, Louis J. A., *The Challenge of Humanism* (Oxford Press, 1933).
Meynell, Alice, *Mary, the Mother of Jesus* (Medici Society, 1932).
Montalembert, Charles Forbes Rene de Tryon, comte de, *Monks of the West* (T. B. Noonan and Co., Boston, 1860, 2 vol.).
Moody, John, *The Long Road Home* (Macmillan, 1933).
Morton, J. B., *Sobieski* (Eyre and Spottiswoode, 1931).

Noyes, Alfred, *The Torchbearers*, An Epic of Science (Stokes, 1922–25, 3 vol.).

O'Hagan, Thomas, *The Genesis of Christian Art* (Macmillan, 1926).

Papini, G., *St. Augustine* (Harcourt, Brace, 1930).
Psichari, Ernest, *A Soldier's Pilgrimage* (Benziger Bros.).

Rand, *Founders of the Middle Ages* (Harvard U. Press, 1928).
Repplier, Agnes, *Mere Marie of the Ursulines* (Macmillan, 1931).
———— *Pere Marquette* (Doubleday, Doran, 1929).

Shuster, G. N., *The Catholic Spirit in Modern English Literature* (Macmillan, 1922).
Stoddard, J. L., *Rebuilding a Lost Faith* (Kenedy, 1921).

———— *Twelve Years in the Catholic Church* (Burns, Oates and Washbourne, 1930).

Stourton, Alison, *Regina Poetarum* (Washbourne, 1907).

Thurston, Herbert, S.J., *No Popery!* (Sheed and Ward, 1930).

Von Hildebrand, Dietrich, *In Defense of Purity* (Sheed and Ward, 1931).

Walsh, Edmund A., S.J., *The Last Stand* (Little, Brown & Co., 1931).

———— *The Fall of the Russian Empire* (Little, Brown & Co., 1928).

Walsh, James J., *The Thirteenth, the Greatest of Centuries* (Catholic Summer School Press, 1907).

Walsh, William T., *Isabella of Spain* (R. M. McBride & Co., 1930).

Wasmann, Eric, S.J., *Christian Monism* (Herder, 1923).

Williams, Michael, *Catholicism and the Modern Mind* (Dial Press, 1928).

———— *The High Romance* (Macmillan, 1926).

Windle, Bertram C. A., *The Catholic Church and Its Reactions with Science* (Calvert Series) (Macmillan, 1927).

———— *The Church and Science* (Herder, 1917).

———— *Twelve Catholic Men of Science* (Catholic Truth Society, 1912).

Yeo, Margaret, *St. Francis Xavier* (Sheed and Ward, 1931).